Personalism
and
Scholasticism

Personalism and Scholasticism

by

John Cowburn, S.J.

Marquette Studies in Philosophy
No. 40
Andrew Tallon, Series Editor

Library of Congress Cataloging-in-Publication Data

Cowburn, John.
  Personalism and scholasticism / John Cowburn.
    p. cm.—(Marquette studies in philosophy ; no. 40)
  Includes bibliographical references and index.
  ISBN-13: 978-0-87462-663-6 (pbk. : alk. paper)
  ISBN-10: 0-87462-663-3 (pbk. : alk. paper)
  1. Scholasticism—History. 2. Personalism—History. 3.
Philosophical theology—History. 4. Theology, Doctrinal—
History. I. Title. II. Series.
  B839.C38 2005
  149'.91—dc22
                                        2005006136

© 2005 Marquette University Press
All rights reserved.

Cover photo by Andrew J. Tallon, 2002
Ourscamp, France, Cistercian Abbey

MARQUETTE UNIVERSITY PRESS
MILWAUKEE

The Association of Jesuit University Presses

Foreword

This book is highly personal and I shall begin by saying who I am. I was born in Australia in 1927 and I entered the Society of Jesus in 1945. In 1947-49 (three years) I was taught Thomistic philosophy and was good at it. I then studied physics at Melbourne University and obtained a science degree. In the late nineteen-fifties I studied theology in Innsbruck and in the sixties I studied post-graduate philosophy in Louvain and Innsbruck, where I wrote a thesis on love. During this time, besides Karl Rahner's theology I discovered Martin Buber and Personalism. At first I added the new to the old, and in my thesis and in a book, *Love and the Person* (published in 1967), I proposed a synthesis of Thomism and Personalism. This helped a number of scholastically-trained people to accept personalist ideas, precisely because it did not ask them to reject Scholasticism, only to add Personalism to it. When in the sixties and seventies I taught philosophy, I found myself using Scholasticism less and less and I came to see defects in it. These have become more and more clear to me and this book is the result of long reflection on them. I have just produced another book on love, called *Love*, which reflects a mind-set somewhat different from the one which I had forty years ago. Firm believers who lose their faith in an intellectual system of any kind often become its fiercest opponents and it is possible that I have gone this way, but I have tried to be fair. I expect it to be said that I have caricatured Scholasticism, or that what I say is true only of the most primitive "school Scholasticism"; in reply to this I ask the reader to study the quotations which I give, which come from Thomas Aquinas, to whom I often refer as Thomas, and leading twentieth-century scholastic thinkers, and to judge them for himself or herself. I give some quotations in Latin in the notes so that anyone who doubts my translations can read the originals. Also, I give many cross-references so that anyone who reads only a passage here or there, in which I deal with some topic in which he or she is interested, can find other passages which deal with it.

John Cowburn, S.J.
Jesuit Theological College
Parkville, Victoria, Australia
29 August 2004

Contents

PART I:
INTRODUCTION AND SHORT HISTORIES OF SCHOLASTICISM AND PERSONALISM

CHAPTER 1: PHILOSOPHY AND THEOLOGY 17
What is philosophy 17
Spectator-philosophy and agent-philosophy 18
Arts-faculty philosophy and science-faculty philosophy 20
Low and high philosophy 21
Some history 22
    Ages in Western culture from around 1100 AD 22
    Philosophy (and some theology) in the ages 24
Takeovers 25

CHAPTER 2: A SHORT HISTORY OF SCHOLASTICISM ... 27
In the Middle Ages 27
In the "Modern Age" 29
    Second Scholasticism 29
    Protestant Scholasticism 31
    The Catholic Church in the 17th & 18th centuries 31
Revival in the Catholic Church 32
Philosophies used in the Church: Traditionalism, Ontologism . 32
Neo-Scholasticism to 1878: the beginning 33
Liberal Catholics in the nineteenth century 35
Leo XIII becomes pope in 1878 36
The Modernists 37
The triumph of Neo-Scholasticism 38
How the dream of unity faded before Vatican II 40
Transcendental Thomism 42
The end of Neo-Scholasticism 44
    Prior to Vatican II 44

  Vatican II 44
  The present situation 44
  Conclusion 46

CHAPTER 3: A HISTORY OF PERSONALISM 47
  "The person" in the world at large: non-personalist use of
    the word 47
  The person in 18th and 19th century continental philosophy 49
    Schleiermacher 49
    Kant 49
    Kierkegaard 50
    Developments in Germany, leading to Personalism 51
    France 51
  Personalism in England and Scotland before World War I 51
  Personalism in the United States 53
    Before Borden Parker Bowne 53
    Borden Parken Bowne and Boston Personalism 54
  Personalist ideas 55
    Personalism in general 56
    Boston Personalism 56
  Twentieth-century Personalism in Germany and France 57
    In Germany, Max Scheler 57
    From Germany to France 59
    In France, Mounier to World War II 60
  Mounier's Personalism in Poland and the United States 63
  Differences between Boston and Mounier Personalisms 64
  Mounier's Personalism in the Catholic Church before WW2 ... 64
  Mounier's and Polish Personalism during WW2 65
  Personalism in the Catholic Church during WW2 66
  Personalism immediately after WW2 67
  Personalism and Existentialism 68
  Personalism in the English-speaking world after WW2 69
    In philosophy departments of universities 69
    Psychologists 72
    The wider English-speaking world 72

Personalism in the Catholic Church after WW2 73
   Immediately after WW2 73
   Lublin Personalism and Karol Wojtyla 73
   Vatican II 75
   After Vatican II to 1978 76
   From 1978 76
Some important religious thinkers and Personalism 77
   Martin Buber 77
   Jacques Maritain 78
   Pierre Teilhard de Chardin 80
   Gabriel Marcel 82
   Bernard Lonergan 83
   Karl Rahner 83

PART II:
SCHOLASTIC PHILOSOPHY AND PERSONALISM

CHAPTER 4: THE TWO PHILOSOPHIES IN GENERAL 87
SCHOLASTICISM 87
Being 87
The four causes 87
Act and potency in Scholasticism 88
The love of unity 88
   The unity of being 89
   Unity in causation 90
The other transcendentals 91
Material beings 92
   Substantial form and matter 92
   The principle of individuation 92
The human being 92
   The definition 92
   Human nature 93
   The intellect and the will 93
   Neo-Scholastics and "the person" 93
PERSONALISM 95
What the person means in Personalism 95

    Likenesses.. 97
    Differences.. 97
    Some differences 97
    Spectator and agent philosophies 98
    The question of historical sense... 98

CHAPTER 5: OBJECTIVE REALITY & SUBJECTIVITY 101
    Introduction 101
        What these terms mean 101
        The room analogy: outside and inside......................... 102
    The connections between object and subject 103
    The study of subjectivity.. 103
    Opposing preferences... 103
    Cases where the distinction is made 105
    Neo-Scholasticism.. 105
    Personalism 106
    That person is higher than being... 108

CHAPTER 6: FREE WILL 109
    What free will is 109
    Free will in Second Scholasticism 110
Neo-Scholasticism 111
    Critism of Neo-Scholasticism 112
Personalism 112

CHAPTER 7: VALUE 113
    Introduction 113
    Scholastic value-theory.. 114
    The value of being and the primary value.......................... 114
        That value is in the whole 114
        Intellectualism 115
        Inequality or grades of being... 116
    Disvalue.. 117
Criticism of Scholastic value-theory 117
Personalist value-theory.. 118
The one and the many in the two philosophies 119

CHAPTER 8: LOVE 121
Scholastic philosophy 121
   The main theory 121
      Secondary ideas 123
   Dominance 123
   Personalists and love 124
   A view which combines both theories 126

CHAPTER 9: ETHICS 127
Scholasticism 127
   In general 127
      Sexual morality 128
      Ownership 128
   Socio-political issues 128
Personalism 129
   A Personalist criticism of Neo-Scholastic ethics 129
   Moral evil 131

PART III: THEOLOGY

CHAPTER 10: SCHOLASTICISM & PERSONALISM 135
The person in theology 135
   Theology in general 137
   First phase: believing what is in the Bible 137
      That there should be a second phase 139
   Using a philosophy 140
   The use of philosophy in the past 140
Using a philosophy now 141
   Systematic theology and religious spirituality 143
Conclusion 145

CHAPTER 11: THE TRINITY 147
The doctrine 147
The psychological theory 149
Scholasticism: Anselm 150
   Criticism of this theory 151

    Richard of St Victor 151
    More recent speculation 151
  Appropriation 153

CHAPTER 12: GOD TO US 155
THE SCHOLASTIC THEORY 155
  Some metaphysical ideas 155
    God as prime mover 155
    That God has total control of events 155
    That God wills the whole 156
    The one divine decision 158
  The problem of non-moral "evil" 159
  The divine non-passivity 159
    That God is pure act 159
    The divine knowledge of creatures 159
    The divine purpose 160
    The divine impassibility 161
    God's love of creatures 163
  The indwelling 164
CRITICISM OF THIS PERFECT-BEING THEOLOGY 164
  The idea of control 165
  Divine knowledge 166
  The divine non-sympathy 167
  The indwelling 168

CHAPTER 13: HUMAN PERSONS TO GOD 169
  Faith 169
    Two conceptions of faith 169
    The freedom and certainty of faith 172
    The approach to faith 173
  Hope and charity: our love of God 173
  Grace and the sacraments 175
  Prayer 176
  Heaven 177

Table of Contents 13

CHAPTER 14: SIN ... 179
What sin is ... 179
- The Neo-Scholastic ideas of divine control and optimism ... 180
- Foreknowledge of immoral acts ... 183
- Impassibility in this context ... 183
    - The stories of two men ... 185
- Conclusion ... 186

CHAPTER 15: HUMAN BEINGS TO EACH OTHER ... 189
- Love of the neighbour ... 189
    - The scholastic theory ... 189
    - Another theory ... 190
    - That charity is not a separate love ... 190
- The Church ... 190
- Ecumenism ... 192

CHAPTER 16: CONCLUSION ... 195
- Being and person ... 195
- Reduction ... 195
- Some statements ... 197

BIBLIOGRAPHY ... 199

INDEX OF NAMES ... 209

INDEX OF SUBJECTS ... 213

Part 1

Philosophy and Theology
and
Short Histories
of
Scholasticism and Personalism

Chapter 1

Some Notes on Philosophy and Theology

At the risk of seeming to be working at an elementary level, before coming to Scholasticism and Personalism I am going to talk fairly generally about philosophy, especially in the Catholic Church.

What is philosophy?

Faculties of philosophy teach different kinds of philosophy and as a general rule each faculty teaches its students that what the faculty is studying is what philosophy is. In some universities, just as the course in English literature consists in lectures on the English literary classics, so the course in philosophy consists in lectures on the European classic philosophical books. The students are taught, either expressly or implicitly, that philosophy is the content of these books, so that to have done philosophy means that you have read them and can talk about them. Elsewhere, philosophers analyse language and define philosophy as linguistic analysis. As we shall see, scholastic philosophers studied being qua being and defined philosophy as precisely that study. It is therefore difficult to give a general definition of philosophy. However, a common feature of all kinds of philosophy is that, in contemporary terms, it is a secular pursuit, at least in the sense that it does not consist in studying what God has revealed through the Biblical writers or in any other special way. When the philosopher has no religious faith, it is "pure" philosophy.

Philosophies usually have names. Some, like Ancient Greek Philosophy, are named after a time and place. Others, like Platonism, Cartesianism (after Descartes) and Thomism, are named after authors, in which case they usually have books to which references are constantly made and they have more unity than philosophies which are named in other ways. Some philosophies, like materialism and subjectivism, are named after particular theories. Some are named after a particular theme or interest: for instance, Existentialism is about existence, by which is meant life (not in the biological sense but in the sense of the word in "a life well lived"). Finally, some philosophies, including Analytical Philosophy, are named after a particular method or style. I am going to be discussing two philosophies which have different kinds of name: Scholasticism is so called because it began in schools which appeared in the twelfth century and because it uses the method or style which was customary in those schools. If the people who gave it its name had used our language, they would probably have called it Academic Philosophy. Personalism is so called because it insists on the value of the person and involves constant use of that word.

Spectator philosophy and agent philosophy

I believe that we can distinguish in a very general way between two different kinds of philosophy

When we see something for the first time, we may ask questions about it. Simple observation answers these up to a point and science takes us further; beyond that we go into philosophy, and some philosophies are cosmic theories, about all of reality or being; or we go into religion. Thought of this kind, if it is not religious, is "spectator philosophy" because it endeavours to answer the questions of an initially puzzled *observer*.

Philosophies of another kind arise when people ask about the meaning of life. If they arrive at conclusions, these become their "philosophies of life". They can be found in the Wisdom books of the Old Testament, the writings of stoics and epicureans, *The Rubáiyat of Omar Khayyám* and the ruminations of what Americans used to call "cracker-barrel philosophers". When people talk about being philosophical or about accepting something philosophically, they have this kind of philosophy vaguely in mind, and if philosophy is a search for wisdom it surely deserves the name. In 1953, when French Existentialism was becoming fashionable in England, E. C. Allen said that it could be defined as "an attempt to philosophise from the standpoint of the actor instead of, as has been customary, from the standpoint of the

Chapter 1: *Philosophy & Theology* 19

spectator".[1] To this I would say, first, that Existentialism was indeed an actor or agent rather than a spectator philosophy, but that this is not a good definition of Existentialism because it applies to hundreds of other philosophies; second, spectator philosophy may have been customary in philosophy departments in England but in the world at large philosophy from the standpoint of the agent has been at least as common. In *Fides et Ratio* John Paul II says that philosophy "is directly concerned with asking the question of life's meaning" (# 2) and that it is "patient inquiry into what makes life worth living" (# 6); its theme, he says, is "the ultimate purpose of personal existence" (# 15); it asks "the fundamental questions which pervade human life" and "the answer given to these questions decides the direction which people seek to give to their lives" (# 1). For him, clearly, agent philosophy *is* philosophy.

As a rule, an agent is more emotionally involved in any enterprise than is a spectator, and books by Kierkegaard, Scheler and Existentialists are more emotionally charged than are those of spectator philosophers, which is one reason why, when translations of French Existentialists appeared in English, many British and other philosophers disdainfully dismissed them as outpourings of emotion, not reason. There are, however, emotional undercurrents in many utterances and writings of spectator philosophers, while many agent philosophers show that it is possible to be emotionally involved in an inquiry and perfectly rational. The difference between spectator and agent philosophy is not, therefore, based on the distinction between reason and emotion.

Kant went so far as to write books of pure and practical reason, or spectator and agent philosophy, and they were not only separate but mutually contradictory. When we are engaged in pure reason, he said in effect, we work with certain suppositions, one of which is determinism, but when we are using practical reason we have suppositions which are the opposite of these, one of which is that we have free will. In contemporary terms, it is as if our brains are like computers which have two programs in them, which we use for different tasks; when we are speculating we use one program, when we are thinking about life we send that program back into the memory and call up the other

---

[1] Allen, *Existentialism From Within*, p. 3. Copleston quotes this in *Contemporary Philosophy*, pp. 127-128.

one. Their incompatibility does not prevent their co-existence in our heads. This dualism is to be found in thinkers who in their articles and lectures deny value judgements and free will, but in their lives constantly make value judgements and assume that they and others have free will.

Just as many theoretical physicists look down on engineers, who are interested in theory only in so far as it can be put to practical use, and theoretical chemists look down on the writers of cookbooks, who are not scientists whatever else they may be, so practitioners of spectator philosophy often despise agent philosophy, make scornful remarks about "therapeutic philosophy" or "save-the-world philosophy", and maintain that it is not really philosophy at all. On the other hand, when practical philosophy, to use Kant's term, is understood as thought about the meaning of life, the value of love and the right attitude to death, pure spectator philosophy can seem to be a frivolous game played by people who are taking a holiday from life.

Arts-faculty and science-faculty philosophy

We are accustomed to a sharp division between "the arts" and "the sciences", and our universities have separate arts and science faculties, which may be said to have different cultures. Philosophy is usually in the arts faculty but many philosophers feel more at home with scientists than with members of the arts faculty. For instance, Terry Pinkard said of Bertrand Russell:

> The young Russell was quite clear in his ambition to make philosophy into a rigorous science that could take its place alongside the other sciences in the university and could proudly say that, just like physics, it had finally solved certain problems and was now working on solutions to others.[2]

An older Russell said in 1953 that his kind of philosophy was able, "in regard to certain problems, to achieve definite answers, which have the quality of science rather than of philosophy".[3] W. V. O. Quine, a philosophy professor at Harvard who was influenced by Russell, said in 1970 that it is "a wing of science where aspects of method are

---

[2] Pinkard, "Analytics, Continentals and Modern Scepticism", p. 191.
[3] Russell, *A History of Western Philosophy*, p. 862.

examined."[4] All of which leads me to say that there now exists a kind of philosophy that is consciously scientific in its method and style. It is usually impersonal.

On the other hand, among the great philosophical books are the dialogues of Plato, which are highly literary. In fact, much agent philosophy has been written in literary forms of various kinds, the Existentialists like Sartre showed little or no awareness of science, and there are thousands of philosophers who, without being hostile in any way to science or ignorant of it, are happy to go on working in arts faculties. It is common for scientifically-minded philosophers to dismiss these philosophers as soft, dreamy, emotional, romantic and irrational. They, for their part, feel sorry for the scientific philosophers, as music-lovers feel sorry for people who have no appreciation of music and do not know what they are missing.

High and low philosophy

It is also possible to distinguish, in a broad way, between high and low streams of both spectator and agent philosophy. By a "low" philosophy I do not here mean one that is of low intellectual level. I mean one that is hard, practical, down-to-earth, unromantic, somewhat materialistic and often morally indulgent or "permissive". By a "high" philosophy I mean one that includes belief in spiritual reality and has demanding ethical principles. I admit that these terms express value judgements.

In ancient Greece, Democritus was a low philosopher. After the Renaissance, low philosophers included David Hume and the British Empiricists, the continental materialists such as Julien La Mettrie, who wrote *Man a Machine* (1747), and the eighteenth-century Encyclopedists, who attacked religion and the accepted moral code. In the twentieth century they included the Logical Positivists, who ridiculed all talk of spiritual realities and values. Low philosophies have also included the Playboy Philosophy and Ayn Rand's Objectivism, which is to be found in her novels and in *The Virtue of Selfishness,* which is subtitled *A New Concept of Egoism*. These philosophies are about as low as it is possible to get.

[4] Quine, "Philosophical Progress in Language Theory", *Metaphilosophy* 1(1970)1, quoted in Midgley, *Information and Wonder,* p. 111.

Low philosophies are generally anti-religious and when religious believers meet one they usually want to have nothing to do with it and they warn their fellow-believers to avoid it. Paul took this attitude towards the low philosophies which he met in Athens and I cannot imagine a Christian feeling anything but distaste for the Playboy Philosophy.

In ancient Greece some intelligent and highly moral men, understandably, ceased to believe in the power-hungry and lustful gods and goddesses of the state religion. They did not adopt other religions and they did not invent new ones, but they thought about life and reality and arrived at some noble or high beliefs about morality, about life before and after death, and about realities which in some sense are above the material world which they saw around them. They sought for a non-religious wisdom and they are now honoured as philosophers. The greatest among them were Plato (ca. 428 to ca. 348 BC) and Aristotle (384-322 BC, hence about forty years younger). Of the two, Plato was the more literary, unworldly, imaginative and fantastic. Aristotle was more realistic, down-to-earth and scientific, but he was not low.

In Parts I and II of this book I shall be concerned mainly with philosophy but as scholastic philosophy was almost entirely an officially Catholic enterprise it would be artificial to omit all reference to religion. I shall therefore say now that when Christian believers discovered high philosophers, they often respected them and saw a certain affinity between their beliefs and their own. For instance, when some early Christians found the dialogues of Plato, they admired Socrates and saw resemblances between him and Christ. Christians also sometimes "used" these philosophies in their search for understanding of their own beliefs, and they were influenced by them. We shall see examples of this.

Some history
Ages in Western European culture from around 1100 AD
Starting with the Middle Ages, Western European history has involved periods, between which there were not sharp breaks, such as occur when at midnight one millenium ends and another begins. Instead, changes of period were more like the slow dissolves in films, when as

Chapter 1: *Philosophy & Theology*

one image dominates the screen the beginnings of another can at first be seen faintly, this second image becomes clearer and the first image fades until finally the first image has gone and the second image is the only one on the screen. In this way, as a certain ensemble of ideas and institutions was dominant, new things appeared in a small way; these developed, the earlier forms lost their dominance, and a new age came in.

In the time of the ancient Greeks and Romans, power was in the hands of people who had a high culture and who dominated, and kept order in, much of Europe. Then barbaric tribes overran most of Europe and what are called the Dark Ages began. In the centuries which followed, there were hundreds of languages and Latin, the language of the old imperial power, was used for high purposes. Christianity survived in pockets.

I begin my story around the year 1100 AD, when, if I may put it this way, civilisation emerged from barbarism and what are called the Middle Ages began. This, of course, was the age of Romanesque and then Gothic architecture, of great painting and sculpture, and of vitality in the Church. This age seems to have reached a high point in the thirteenth century, when the greatest Gothic cathedrals were built and the Dominican and Franciscan orders were founded. It declined in the fourteenth and fifteenth centuries.

When the Middle Ages were declining, new things appeared which eventually became dominant, and a new age began. This is often called "The Modern Age". It included printing, a new financial system and the appearance of vernacular languages as unified languages which could be used for "high" purposes. A new architectural style, which began with small, simple buildings, appeared and became fashionable. In the sixteenth century came the Reformation and the Counter-Reformation. These included the Council of Trent, at which the Catholic Church "updated" itself. Some vernacular languages had golden ages. Towards the end of the sixteenth century and early in the seventeenth, Shakespeare wrote his plays and the King James Bible was published. In these two centuries the solar system was discovered and written about, Newton discovered gravitation and classical or Newtonian physics was born. Also, some great European empires came into being.

I for one am inclined to believe that we have moved from the Modern Age into another one, which I shall call the Present Age. There is a new physics, which has replaced Newtonian physics; there is a different picture of the universe; there have been immense advances in technology and there were changes in art and a new style of architecture, which again began with small, simple buildings, appeared. The empires vanished. Big countries such as Germany and the United States have become far more united than they used to be and different countries have united to form entities like the United Nations and the European Union. The various Christian churches have become co-operative with one another. In the Catholic Church, Vatican II (1962-65) can be seen as the council in which the Church situated itself in this Present Age, which it called "the world of this time".

Philosophy (and some theology) in the ages

As I said, in about the fourth century BC Plato and Aristotle flourished. After them there was a decline and about four hundred years later, or in the first century AD, Philo, a Greek-speaking Jew in Alexandria, studied Aristotle and endeavoured to produce a sort of Aristotelian Judaism. From this came an Aristotelian tradition in the Arab world, which was separate from the Greek and Roman worlds.

In the time of the Roman Empire, when most of Europe was in the power of cultured people, Christians discussed and wrote about their beliefs, first in Greek and then in Latin, so that the makings of a vast theological library came into being. The authors who wrote before the Fall of the Roman Empire are known as the Fathers of the Church.

In the third century AD, Plotinus appeared. Though he was of Roman parentage and settled in Rome when he was about forty, his language was Greek. He was influenced by Plato and when he died a pupil of his published the *Enneads,* in which his philosophy, which came to be known as Neo-Platonism, was expressed. This had a great vogue in the Greek and Roman worlds and it influenced Augustine, who was a pagan philosopher until he became a Christian in 386 AD.

As the name indicates, there was not much philosophical or theological thought in Western Europe in the Dark Ages, but Christianity survived in pockets. At least some people there could read Latin and naturally they were much more strongly influenced by Augustine than by the Fathers of the Church who had written in Greek.

I will pass over the Dark Ages and also, because I am going to write about medieval philosophy in the next chapter, the Middle Ages.

In 1637, which is to say in the Modern Age, Descartes published his *Discourse on Method,* in which he proposed starting philosophy again from one certain truth, which would be, he said, "I think, therefore I am", or "I, who am a thinking subject, exist". This was so much in the spirit of the age that the book was immediately a huge success and "I think, therefore I am" became a kind of slogan. Descartes is now regarded as the father of modern (as opposed to medieval) philosophy. The high philosophy of this age ended in the nineteenth century in subjectivism, or the belief that what we think is "outer" reality is all "in the mind", so that when we study physics we are actually studying the workings of the human mind, just as when we talk about complementary colours we are actually talking about how the human brain works. The high philosophy of this age was not on the whole clearly opposed to the churches but it was mainly outside them.

Starting in the nineteenth century, some philosophers discovered "the other person", as subject, and John Cullberg has said that awarness of "the Thou" led to the abandonment of subjectivism.[5] In 1923 Martin Buber published *I and Thou* in Vienna and the phrase "I and Thou" became a sort of slogan of the Present Age, rather as Descartes's "I think, therefore I am" had been a slogan of the Modern Age.

Takeovers

At times an academic field is the scene of a dispute between two factions and in a particular university or national association one faction becomes dominant. Let us suppose, for instance, purely by way of example, that in a particular country psychologists are divided into Freudians and others and that Freudians obtain control of university psychology faculties and the national psychological association. In the universities, Jungian and other lecturers find themselves teaching small classes at odd times and being ostracised in the common rooms, until they resign and are replaced by Freudians. Good students who

---

[5] Cullberg, *Das Du und die Wirklichkeit (The Thou and Reality),* pp. 25-34.

are natural Freudians obtain high marks for their essays and some of them go on to pursue academic careers, whereas other equally good students obtain lower marks and switch to other fields. At meetings of the national association all the main papers are given by Freudians and either no others speak or a few other papers are read in out-of-the-way venues at awkward times. To attract attention at the meetings, which they need to do in order to obtain good positions, to attract funding for research, and to get their work published, psychologists need to be Freudians. From this it cannot be concluded either that only Freudianism is right or that it is the only right system for a particular country or for people who speak a particular language..

Chapter 2

A Short History of Scholasticism[1]

The Middle Ages

The cultural revival of the twelfth century included in Western Europe an intellectual movement which was highly rational. An early figure in it was Anselm of Canterbury, who said in effect that we need not only to believe but also to understand what we believe, which is not the same thing. People began to think systematically, with clearly defined terms and logical arguments, looking for intellectually satisfying explanations. This usually meant looking for a complete general theory of reality: particular things could then be explained by "placing" them in it. This caught on. Schools in which rational speculation was practised appeared in France and elsewhere. In these schools the teaching and writing were in Latin, which had the advantage that it was used everywhere, so that in spite of the difficulty of travelling there was an international intellectual world, with an agreed style. I will not describe this style here, except to say that it was thorough and laborious, not to say tedious, and that it went with the name "scholastic", so that when one talks now of Scholastic Philosophy one thinks not so much of the schools in which it was originally taught, and from which it got its name, as of the style in which, then and later, it was expressed. As I will later say, the teachers in the medieval schools differed so much from each other that their theories constituted different philosophies, but because of the method which they shared, the general term, "Scholastic Philosophy", covers all of them.

---

[1] Especially when dealing with Second Scholasticism and Neo-Scholasticism, I shall make use of Gerard McCool, *Nineteenth-Century Scholasticism* (1977), its sequel *From Unity to Pluralism: The Internal Evolution of Thomism* (1989) and *The Neo-Thomists* (1994). I shall also use Emerich Coreth, "Schulrichtungen neuscholastischer Philosophie" (1988).

In the middle of the twelfth century Peter the Lombard produced four books of *Sententiae*, which means "Beliefs and opinions", in which he set out, in logical order, views on the main topics of theology. Almost everywhere teachers used these books in class, following their order and in some cases writing commentaries on them, and they were used in this way for centuries.

Many of the beliefs of Scholastic thinkers were what was generally known (or thought) at the time: they believed in the reality of the world we see, in causality, in free will and in morality; they also thought that the world was flat, that the sun moves across the sky, and so on. Other beliefs were "general Christian": they believed in the existence of God, the Trinity, the divinity of Christ, the inspiration of the scriptures, the Church, the immortality of the soul and redemption through Christ's suffering and death. Their ideas had come from before the Dark Ages and to a large extent they had come from Augustine, and via him from Neo-Platonism and via it from Plato. However, the Moors from North Africa had invaded Spain, they had made Aristotle known to Christians there and the knowledge had spread to other countries. As a result, an Aristotelian movement, which was more down-to-earth and rational than the Platonist tradition, had appeared in various parts of Europe. To use present-day terms, those who professed a Platonist Christianity were conservatives and they were highly suspicious of the progressive Aristotelians, who ran into opposition.

A leading Aristotelian Christian was Thomas Aquinas (1225-74), who discovered Aristotle's works in Naples, which was a Spanish possession, and wrote commentaries on them. For the rest of his life he referred to Aristotle as "the philosopher" and he reasoned like a Christian Aristotle. An early work of his was a commentary on the *Sententiae* of Peter the Lombard but towards the end of his life he wrote the *Summa Theologica*, a long, closely reasoned book about virtually every theological question he could think of. On every question, he took a definite position and one is aware of an independent, synthetic mind at work. Judged historically, it is one of the greatest intellectual achievements of Western civilisation.

Because of Thomas's Aristotelianism, after his death in 1274 conservatives opposed the spread of his ideas. In 1277 the bishop of Paris condemned some propositions which included several that were from

Chapter 2: *A Short History of Scholasticism* 29

him and he was also condemned by the Dominican Archbishop of Canterbury. However, in 1279 the Dominican chapter declared that it was in favour of him, in 1313 the order made him its official teacher, and in 1323 he was canonised by Pope John XXII, who said that one could learn more by reading his books for a year than by reading the works of others for a lifetime. Nevertheless, Peter the Lombard's *Sententiae* remained the book on which teachers based their lectures.

The next centuries saw what has been called "the waning of the Middle Ages". There were many wars, court dress became over-elaborate, Gothic buildings were decorated with complicated stonework, a certain scepticism and almost despair became widespread and there was much corruption in the Church. The Franciscan Duns Scotus (ca 1265-1303; therefore he was about nine when Thomas died) proposed a new and (may I say?) rather fantastic system, which for a time was widely accepted in his order. About twenty years later another Franciscan, William of Ockham, proposed a rather low philosophy that is called "nominalism" and this caught on, so that after a time Thomas and Scotus were hardly known and nominalism was the mainstream movement in philosophy. If the philosophers of the time did not actually discuss how many angels can stand on the point of a pin, most of their speculation was as irrelevant as that would have been and good men were contemptuous of it. Thus, with the culture as a whole, medieval Scholasticism came to an inglorious end.

Scholasticism in the "Modern Age" which came after the Middle Ages and ended in the twentieth century

Second Scholasticism

Around 1500 there was an intellectual and spiritual revival in the Dominican order and later there was a burst of Scholastic activity in Spain, where the Jesuits Suarez and Vasquez wrote important books; where the Dominican Bañez wrote; and where, half a century later, the Dominican John of St Thomas taught and wrote. Thus, after the cynicism and despair of the late Middle Ages, what has been called Second Scholasticism came with refreshing, positive force. It flourished until around 1650 and it had four characteristics which were new.

First, Thomas Aquinas came to be regarded as far and away the greatest medieval Scholastic author. In the first half of the sixteenth century Dominicans in various places began to follow his *Summa* instead of Peter the Lombard's *Sententiae* in their courses, and this caught on. Ignatius Loyola, who was influenced by Dominicans when he studied in Paris from 1528 to 1535, said in the Jesuit *Constitutions* (published in 1558), concerning the studies of Jesuits: "There should be lectures on the Old and New Testaments and on the scholastic doctrine of St Thomas" (# 464), and the Jesuit Robert Bellarmine is quoted as having said that one could learn more by studying St Thomas for two months than by devoting many years to the study of the scriptures and the Fathers of the Church.

Second, printing had been invented around 1440 and, instead of explaining Aristotle, Thomas Aquinas or other classical authors whose works the students could consult in the library, lecturers produced printed textbooks in which they set out their interpretations of those authors. Then and in the centuries which followed, most students studied these textbooks, only rarely consulting the classical authors.

Third, unlike Thomas and other medieval writers, the Second Scholastics wrote separate books of philosophy and theology. For instance, Suarez wrote *Disputationes Metaphysicae,* distinct from his books of theology, and John of St Thomas wrote a *Cursus Philosophicus Thomisticus*[2] distinct from his *Cursus Theologicus*. However, the Scholastic Philosophy and Theology of this period were closely linked, as both were predominantly clerical enterprises.

Fourth, there were different schools of Scholastic Philosophy, each associated with a religious order. On the one hand, the authority of Thomas was paramount. On the other hand, authors endeavoured not merely to understand his thought but also to develop it, and the various religious orders interpreted him in different ways. Each order taught its own philosophy in its own schools and for the most part they went their separate ways, which was just as well since the loyalty of each order to its own system and its hostility to other systems was

---

[2] The full title of the philosophy course, translated into English, is *Thomistic Philosophy Course, according to the Exact, True and Genuine Mind of Aristotle and the Angelic Doctor.* By the Angelic Doctor he meant Thomas and one sees here the option for Aristotle rather than Plato.

Chapter 2: *A Short History of Scholasticism* 31

intense. Dominican authors, especially John of St Thomas, developed what came to be called Thomism and was taught in Dominican schools. In the Society of Jesus, Suarez, who I am sure believed that he was developing Thomas's thought, not diverging from it, worked out at immense length a system which came to be called Suarezianism and this became the Jesuit orthodoxy. As the Jesuits opened, or took over, many colleges and universities, Suarezianism became the most widespread form of Scholasticism, followed by Thomism and then Scotism.

Protestant Scholasticism and its influence on Catholics

Luther was contemptuous of Aristotle and Scholasticism but around 1600 some Protestant theologians were in many ways like the Catholic Scholastics, whose books they read, and they began to produce textbooks like theirs. Thus, there was such a thing as Protestant Scholasticism.[3]

In 1720 Christian Wolf began to produce, first in German and then in Latin, forty volumes of philosophy which were Scholastic in style. He distinguished between reason and experience, defined philosophy as a work of reason, and aimed to produce a metaphysics logically deduced from first principles. He divided metaphysics into general and special metaphysics; general metaphysics was also called ontology and special metaphysics was divided into cosmology, psychology and theodicy. This was adopted by Catholics, who for more than two centuries gave courses and wrote textbooks on these subjects.

The Catholic Church
in the late seventeenth and eighteenth centuries

According to Coreth, in the late seventeenth century the Jesuits to a large extent abandoned Suarezianism and the period known as Second Scholasticism came to an end. However, the Dominicans held on to Thomism and in 1777 Salvatore Rossi OP produced a Thomistic *Summa Philosophica* which had several editions in Italy and Spain. Also, I am told that in the middle of the eighteenth century the Vincentian college in Piacenza became a scholastic centre and that there

---

[3] See Carl R. Trueman and R. S. Clark, eds., *Protestant Scholasticism: Essays in Reassessment*.

was a revival of Scholastic Philosophy in Barcelona, in which some Jesuits were involved.

I am here writing a short history of Scholasticism, not of philosophy, but to understand the significance of Neo-Scholasticism, to which I am coming, it is important to know that in the eighteenth century there was a widespread rejection of revealed religion and the churches. Deism, or belief in an impersonal divinity which in present-day terms would be thought of as a great unseen computer, was common and so was atheistic rationalism. There was widespread decadence in the Catholic Church and intellectually it was in disarray.

Revival in the Catholic Church

In the nineteenth century there was a revival in the Church, one element of which was the restoration in 1814 of the Society of Jesus, which became, in general, committed to restoration rather than renewal. In 1824 it was again given charge of the Roman College, which was to become the Gregorian University. During the century the Church grew in size, vitality and importance in many countries, including the United States and Ireland, there was a tremendous increase in missionary activity and an amazing number of religious orders were founded. During this time Catholic theologians studied the Fathers of the Church as never before and between 1844 and 1866 Migne in France published their works in almost four hundred uniform volumes. In Tübingen, Germany, a great Catholic school of theology appeared which was mainly biblical and patristic in its approach.[4]

Philosophies used in the Catholic Church: Traditionalism and Ontologism

Obviously enough, to understand and explain Christian beliefs some theologians looked not only to the scriptures, the Fathers of the Church and the accepted world-views of their cultures, but also to the current philosophies. This often meant Cartesian or Kantian philosophy. Others set out in a totally different direction and produced

---

[4] McCool's *Nineteenth-Century Scholasticism*, which was called *Catholic Theology in the Nineteenth Century* when it was first published, contains an account of this pre-Neo-Scholastic theology.

two theories which now strike us as reactionary and, if I may put it this way, excessively pious. One theory was Traditionalism, according to which human reason can find nothing without divine revelation. Traditionalists maintained that the basic truths were revealed to our ancestors and have been passed from generation to generation, so that our principal, or indeed our only, source of truth is tradition. Another was Ontologism, according to which we obtain our knowledge not by observing the things around us but by seeing the divine nature itself. These were taught in many Catholic institutions in France and Italy, respectively, until they were condemned in 1855 and 1866. In 1826 Rosmini began writing and he had a great influence; I shall not attempt to summarise his thought here; I will merely say that he was not a Scholastic philosopher or theologian.

Neo-Scholasticism to 1878: the beginning

Within the general revival, a number of movements appeared in the Church which endeavoured to restore it to health by returning it to the Middle Ages: Gothic architecture, Gregorian chant and medieval monastic liturgy were revived (or, to be more accurate, imitated), quasi-medieval religious communes appeared and some authors wanted to revive the medieval guilds. In the same spirit, in different places people appeared who aimed to restore unity and vitality to the Church's intellectual life by obtaining general or even universal acceptance in it of Scholastic Philosophy and Theology.[5] There was a group of such men in Naples, where the Dominicans had continued to make their young men study Thomas. Also, some of the Jesuits who had been Scholastic thinkers in Barcelona in the eighteenth century had gone to Italy when the Society was banned in Spain and had remained there, promoting Scholasticism, when the Society was suppressed in 1773. Among their intellectual descendants were two Sordi brothers, who entered the Society when it was restored in 1814 and preached Scholasticism in the noviceship, where they converted a certain Taparelli. In Germany, there were Jesuit Scholastic philosophers in Mainz. These included Joseph Kleutgen, who went to work in Rome in 1843.

---

[5] Many Neo-Scholastics object to Neo-Scholasticism being put with Neo-Gothic architecture and Gregorian chant but, let's face it, it was medieval.

Between 1853 and 1860 he wrote *Die Theologie der Vorzeit (The Theology of the Early Time)* in four volumes, in which he maintained that Scholastic Philosophy was the only one in terms of which Christian theologians could work successfully, and in 1860 he produced *Die Philosophie der Vorzeit (The Philosophy of the Early Time)*.

Scholastic Philosophy and Theology appealed to many thinking Catholics for a number of reasons. For one thing, unlike Traditionalism and Ontologism, without being rationalisic it was rational and it was not fantastic, as they were. In a time when subjectivism was strong in university circles, it was realistic. Whereas in the wider educated world there was a widespread worship of science, and people were asked not merely to have faith in it but to hope in it and love it, Scholasticism was spiritual. Moreover, the job of eliminating unchristian elements from Plato and Aristotle had been done and what had come down from Second Scholasticism was impeccably orthodox, whereas theology influenced by modern philosophers was sometimes questionable. Finally, while its proponents claimed that Scholasticism had been for centuries the traditional thought-system of the Church, they aimed to confront contemporary problems, not ignore them. For these reasons, it seemed to many thinking Catholics, especially clerics, that Scholasticism would dispel the darkness in which Catholics had been wandering and they dreamed of making it the philosophy and theology of the Catholic Church. In present-day language, they were the progressives of their time.

At first this intellectual movement had relatively few members but, like the members of the ecumenical and liturgical movements in the twentieth century, the promoters of Scholasticism were determined, energetic, in communication with one another and (as we shall see) ultimately successful. They did not, at first, have an easy run. For instance, in 1829 the Jesuit Taparelli became provincial in Naples, where he appointed a Sordi to teach Scholastic Philosophy. The students rebelled, an investigator was sent from Rome, Sordi was removed and in 1833 Taparelli ceased to be provincial. No doubt the anti-Scholastic protesters celebrated. In 1847 Newman was told by a Jesuit in Rome that Scholasticism was not in favour there and Philip Caraman says that in 1878 most of the professors at the Roman College "did no more than pay Thomas nominal respect".[6]

[6] Caraman, *University of the Nations*, p. 107.

However, when he was rector of the Roman College, Taparelli, working quietly, had converted Carlo Mario Curci, a Jesuit, and Vincenzo Pecci to Scholasticism. In 1850 Pius IX launched the periodical *Civiltá Cattolica,* which he entrusted to the Jesuits, who appointed Curci as editor. Curci recruited other Scholastic Jesuits and in 1853 the periodical began a veritable compaign for Scholasticism. It was helped by Kleutgen and others. In 1854 a Jesuit general congregation was held, at which Taparelli proposed that Jesuits return to fidelity to their constitutions and unite intellectually by adopting "the doctrine of St Thomas", which meant Scholasticism, in all their schools. This proposal was accepted. A group of believers in Scholasticism, including Sordi, Taparelli and Kleutgen, thereupon prepared a Scholastic study handbook complete with rules, and in 1858 Fr General Beckx made this mandatory in the order. The Gregorian faculty did not change its ways, however, and in 1861 a "bitter polemic" began between it and *Civiltá Cattolica.* The general called the two parties together, no agreement was reached but he ordered them to stop attacking one another; they did, and the Gregorian continued for a time on its unscholastic way.

Before 1878, then, while Scholasticism had become a strong (and somewhat intolerant) movement in the Church, freedom existed and by no means all Catholic theologians were Scholastics. Newman, for instance, published his *Essay on the Development of Christian Doctrine* in 1845, the year in which he became a Roman Catholic, and his *Grammar of Assent* in 1870. These were not Scholastic works.

Liberal Catholics in the nineteenth century

During the nineteenth century the ideas of democracy and the secular state gained ground in almost every Western country. Some European Catholics thought, as we do, that the Church should accept these developments: they were called "Liberal Catholics". They were fiercely opposed by other Catholics, whom we would call conservatives: these saw democracy and secular states as evil results of the French Revolution and maintained that "Liberal Catholic" was a contradiction in terms. The popes, especially Pius IX, who reigned from 1846 to 1878, were hostile to the Liberal Catholics. McCool says of the Neo-Scholastics that "none of them claimed to be a democrat" and that they were on the pope's side.

Leo XIII becomes pope in 1878

In 1878 Vincenzo Pecci, who had been converted to Scholasticism by Taparelli, became Pope Leo XIII and in 1879 he issued the encyclical *Aeterni Patris,* which was written entirely or mostly by Kleutgen, in which and by subsequent actions the pope virtually imposed Scholasticism on the Church. Because of orders or pressure from him, at the Gregorian University the anti-Scholastic Palmieri was dismissed, Kleutgen was made the prefect of studies, a new corps of philosophy professors was appointed and the Thomist Louis Billot, who had taught at the Gregorian in 1885-86 and then been sent home to France, was brought back to Rome, where he published a series of highly scholastic books. McCool says that the neo-Thomists were not opposed to the use of force and that "at least one historian has implied that the real explanation of neo-Thomism's triumph over its rivals in the nineteenth century was an unscrupulously brutal use of its authority by a clerical establishment".[7] For instance, Leo XIII made Neo-Scholastics members of various Roman congregations and, urged on by a Scholastic, he condemned forty propositions of Rosmini, who had died in 1853; this effectively finished Rosmini's influence. I am not sure whether this counts as brutal, but Leo XIII made more than a few Scholastics, in Rome and elsewhere, into cardinals. Among them were a certain Mazella, who was a Jesuit, and his own brother, Giuseppe, who had been a Jesuit but who had left the order in 1848. When Giuseppe was in his old age, Leo persuaded him to re-enter the Society of Jesus, which he did, his vows being accepted by Mazella. After Giuseppe died in the following year, 1890, Leo responded to a wish of his by addressing a letter (probably written by Mazella) to the Society in which he ordered it to obey its constitutions and commit itself in perpetuity to Scholasticism (he talked of a *definita et perpetua lex*).

In the United States, the Third Plenary Council of Baltimore, at which the bishops of the country assembled to frame Church legisla-

---

[7] McCool, *Nineteenth-Century Scholasticism*, p. 135. The historian was Pierre Thibault.

tion, was held in 1884. In its decree on seminary training it prescribed Thomas.

In 1887 in Louvain, Cardinal Mercier founded the Neo-Scholastic Institut supérieur de philosophie, where lectures were given and books were written, where future professors from all over the world studied and where some great research was done, much of which was published in the *Revue néo-scholastique de philosophie*.

When the Neo-Scholastic movement first gained momentum, there was a rise in price in antiquarian bookshops of books by early Scholastic authors, some of which had found their way into those shops when religious houses were closed. Later, the writings of Thomas and other medieval authors were edited and published[8] and Second-Scholastic books were reprinted, so that any seminary could have the works of Thomas and others; also, hundreds of textbooks and monographs were published; but this took time.

The Modernists

While Scholasticism was advancing, there were men and at least one woman in the Church who believed that a return to the Middle Ages was not the way to go, in theology or anything else. Without having definite ideas about what this would mean, they believed that the Catholic Church should be "modern". They did not form themselves into an association, which might have organised congresses, but they formed a loose network of like-minded people, between whom and the Neo-Scholastics there was hostility. They were loosely allied with the Liberal Catholics whom I mentioned above.

These people were not opposed to the study of medieval philosophy and theology. Far from it. But one thing in common to all of them was a rejection of the idea that Scholastic Philosophy should be the only philosophy to be taught in the Church's institutions.

In 1903 Leo XIII died and he was succeeded by Pius X, a reactionary pope who in 1907 issued the encyclical *Pascendi*. This was partly written by Mattiussi and it had whole phrases from Billot.[9]

---

[8] There were several editions of Thomas's works and then Leo XIII appointed Zigliara to head a commission which brought out the critical Leonine edition.

It said that "Modernists (as they are commonly and rightly called)" cleverly presented their doctrines in a scattered way, concealing their system, which it proceeded to expound.[10] It then said that there was no surer sign that a man was on his way to Modernism than when he began to show a dislike for Scholasticism. Scholastic Philosophy, it said, must be made the basis of the sacred sciences and those who exalted the study of the Fathers in such a way as to seem to despise Scholasticism were to be disapproved of as of Modernist tendencies and not allowed to teach in seminaries. It said: "The doctorate of theology and canon law must never be conferred on anybody who has not made the regular course of Scholastic Philosophy; if conferred it shall be held as null and void". The encyclical ordered "Councils of Vigilance" to be instituted in all dioceses and it was followed by a veritable persecution of virtually all except Scholastic philosophers and theologians, who, of course, flourished (Billot, for instance, was made a cardinal in 1911 and Mattiussi replaced him as professor of theology at the Gregorian[11]).

The triumph of Neo-Scholasticism

During the anti-modernist "terror"[12] Neo-Scholastic Philosophy had a free run. This continued after Pius X died and was succeeded by the more moderate Benedict XV, and in the Church it took over completely.

---

[9] *Pascendi* said that Kant was the source of modern errors. This probably came from Mattiussi. Others would have said that the trouble began with Descartes or the French Revolution.

[10] If in 1960 someone had published an article on "Progressivism", creating a coherent system out of the most extreme proposals for change which were in circulation at that time and claiming to show that all progressive ideas were derived from the French Revolution (religious liberty being liberty, collegiality being equality and ecumenism being fraternity), which sprang from Enlightenment rationalism, it would have been like *Pascendi*.

[11] For more about Billot, see below, p. 129.

[12] When Bendict XV was elected pope in 1914, Monsignor Mignot, the Archbishop of Albi, wrote to the Secretary of State about "the terror" which had existed in the Catholic world. In France the term "terror" calls to mind the actions of the Committee for Public Safety in France in 1793-94.

Chapter 2: *A Short History of Scholasticism*

In 1917 the *Code of Canon Law* was promulgated and it said that professors of philosophy and theology "shall [i.e., must] adhere religiously to the methods, doctrine and principles of St Thomas". Eventually almost all the faculties controlled by the Roman Catholic Church were teaching Scholastic Philosophy and Theology, separately, theses were being written, doctorates were being awarded, textbooks and monographs were being published, scholarly periodicals were being published and conferences and congresses were being held. Amost all the work was done in medieval (as opposed to classical) Latin by Catholic priests and priests-to-be, who formed an international intellectual community in which almost any scholar could become known everywhere and teach anywhere and any seminarian, once he had learned Latin, could go anywhere and at once attend classes.

Many Neo-Scholastics dreamed of this philosophy becoming the thought-system of the whole Catholic world, uniting it, and, to realise this dream, efforts were made to take Scholastic Philosophy to laypeople. In Louvain, lectures were given in French. Scholastic books were written in French, German, English and other languages. In the United States, obligatory courses in Scholastic Philosophy were taught in English in Catholic colleges. Catholic intellectuals joined study-groups which worked through what they familiarly called "the Summa" and books, such as the one by G. K. Chesterton, were written to promote intellectual devotion to St Thomas Aquinas, with the result that it came to be widely believed that he had been the greatest Catholic thinker of all time and many associations of Catholic university students were called Aquinas Societies.

The Neo-Scholastics generally adopted the Wolffian division of philosophy into the following major subjects: (1) general metaphysics or ontology; (2) cosmology, the study of inorganic beings; (3) psychology, the study of living beings; (4) theodicy or natural theology. To these subjects they added (5) ethics, which was less Scholastic in its style, and (6) critica, also known as major logic and epistemology, the chief purpose of which was to refute subjectivism.

Like Second Scholasticism, only more so, Neo-Scholasticism used printed textbooks. When the duplicator or roneo machine was invented, many professors produced book-length notes for their students. Most professors used a textbook or notes, through which they worked in class and which the students studied in their rooms, rarely consulting the works of Thomas and similar authors in the library.

How the dream of unity faded before Vatican II

When in the nineteenth century the movement to restore Scholastic Philosophy began, its protagonists knew that there had been some disagreements among medieval philosophers and theologians, but they thought that in the Middle Ages there had been general agreement on essentials so that one could talk about medieval philosophy not as one talks about ancient Greek philosophy but as meaning a single philosophy. In the early nineteen-hundreds, Maurice de Wulf of Louvain supported this view by producing a scholarly *History of Mediaeval Philosophy*, in which he talked of a "scholastic synthesis" or common philosophical creed. They also knew that in the time of Second Scholasticism there had been conflicts between Dominican Thomists and Jesuit Suarezians, but they thought that they had agreed on fundamentals. Most of the early Jesuit Neo-Scholastics were Suarezians and when in 1854 the Jesuit general congregation declared that in the Society of Jesus philosophy and theology had to be based on Thomas, this was understood to mean Thomas as interpreted by Suarez, whose complete works were republished in over twenty folio volumes in the eighteen-fifties. It was with this idea of the unity of Scholastic Philosophy that the early Neo-Scholastics dreamt of uniting the Church by means of it and when in 1878 Leo XIII talked of the philosophy of St Thomas, he meant Scholasticism in general, not Thomism as opposed to Suarezianism and Scotism.

Fairly soon, however, it became apparent that there were radical differences between these schools. For the most part, in the beginning the three orders went their separate ways but eventually it became clear that they had different philosophies. There were fierce disputes, in particular between Thomists and Suarezians over the real distinction between essence and existence: the Thomists maintained that the main difference between God and creatures is that essence and existence are identical in God whereas in creatures there is a real distinction between them; the Suarezians denied the real distinction in creatures, which Thomists took to imply that for Suarezians there was no significant

Chapter 2: *A Short History of Scholasticism* 41

difference between God and creatures. Also, Dominicans and Jesuits held opposing views on grace and free will.[13]

Generally speaking, the Dominicans were united in their Thomism and the Franciscans were all Scotists, but some Jesuits, including Billot and Mattiussi, became Thomists so that there was a division in the Society of Jesus.

Some efforts were made to expel Suarezianism and Scotism from the Church. In 1914 Pius X issued *Doctoris Angelici* ("Angelic Doctor" being a title of Thomas Aquinas) and a month later the Congregation for Studies published a statement of "the fundamental points of Thomist philosophy" in twenty-four theses, the third of which was that in creatures there is a real distinction between essence and existence. The evident purpose of the document, which is known as *The Twenty-Four Theses,* was to declare that Thomism, as opposed to Suarezianism and Scotism, was what had been imposed on the Church by Leo XIII. (The Dominican position on free will was not one of the theses, probably because the document was written by Mattiussi.)

This document caused consternation among Suarezians and Scotists. The Jesuit general Martin, who I presume was a Suarezian, asked the Vatican what obligation existed and was told in effect that Jesuits were free to continue to deny the real distinction. In 1915 a Jesuit general congregation was held which elected Ledochowski, who asked the new pope, Benedict XV, if the response which had been given to Martin was still valid, and Benedict told him that it was. In 1916 Ledochowski, who I am sure was also a Suarezian, addressed a long letter to the Society in which he said that a denial of the real distinction was compatible with general adhesion to Thomas. He also said that Jesuit Thomists should not say that it was a basic thesis of Catholic philosophy or that it was necessary for the explanation of any dogmas. The crisis thus passed but in Church circles there was now a cloud over Suarezianism and Scotism while the sun shone on Thomism, so that when in 1917 the *Code of Canon Law* said that professors of philosophy and theology had to "adhere religiously to the methods, doctrines and principles of St Thomas", this made Suarezians

---

[13] See below, p. 110.

and Scotists feel a little unsure of themselves, though canon lawyers assured them that they were in order.[14]

The Vatican seems to have put some pressure on the Gregorian University, where as Suarezian lecturers retired they were replaced by Thomists. Jesuits from many provinces obtained doctorates from the Gregorian, were converted to Thomism, then became lecturers in philosophy or theology in their own countries, with the result that gradually Thomists came to outnumber Suarezians in the Society. Suarezianism, however, continued to be taught by Jesuits in France (or, to be more precise, Jersey), Spain and Austria. The Franciscans were not so divided and they had a number of centres in Italy, Germany and the United States, in which Scotism was taught and the works of the great Franciscans of the past were edited and published.

While all this was going in, work on medieval authors by Etienne Gilson and others after World War I showed that the differences between medieval authors were far more significant than had been thought and the idea of a single medieval philosophy was abandoned.

Transcendental Thomism

There have been three streams which are different but have a kind of family resemblance. All are concerned with intellectual knowledge or the working of the human mind and they all derive from Jesuits who did much work on Thomas Aquinas.

During World War I, in Belgium, Joseph Maréchal (1878-1944) began what became his life's work. At a time when most Neo-Scholastic philosophers dealt with Kant as someone to be refuted, he took him seriously and set about developing the refutation of subjectivism which Thomas Aquinas might have written if he had still been alive. In 1926 Maréchal published in French a book the title of which can be freely translated as *Thomas Aquinas Meets Kant*.[15] The book was

---

[14] The Suarezian Jesuits did not believe that they had been granted an exemption from a law, like the exemption from the law against orchestral Masses which had been granted to the Catholics of Austria and Bavaria. They believed that being true to Thomas, which was obligatory, did not necessarily involve being a Thomist as opposed to a Suarezian.

[15] Maréchal, *Le point de départ de la métaphysique*, Cahier V, *Le Thomisme devant la Philosophie critique*.

Chapter 2: *A Short History of Scholasticism* 43

dismissed by conservative Scholastics but various thinkers, especially Jesuits, were influenced by it and one may say that a stream flowed from it.

In 1936, in Freiburg, Germany, Karl Rahner (1904-84) presented a thesis on knowledge in Thomas. If my information is correct, it was not accepted as a valid interpretation of Thomas, so that he did not obtain a doctorate then, but it was published in 1939 as *Geist in Welt (Spirit in the World)*. In it he acknowledged a debt to Maréchal and later, when it was said that he was influenced by Heidegger, he replied, "No, rather by Maréchal". However, Karl Rahner was not a participant in the stream of Maréchalian discussion which had been and still was going on in French. In Innsbruck after World War II what was called "the transcendental method" appeared. Its chief authors were Emeric Coreth and Otto Muck, who wrote a book whose full title in German means *The Transcendental Method in Present-Day Scholastic Philosophy*. Muck begins the book with chapters on Maréchal.

Bernard Lonergan (1900-1984) was a Canadian Jesuit theologian who studied Thomas on intellection and in 1946-49 produced what are known as the *Verbum* articles, which explain the generation of the second divine person by the first as the intellectual utterance of an inner Word. He subsequently worked on human intellectual knowledge and in 1957 published the philosophical book, *Insight*. This and subsequent writings have had great influence and there is now a Lonerganian stream.

These three streams are sometimes put together as "Transcendental Thomism", though I have been told that Lonergan did not accept the term "transcendental", which in this context has a Kantian sense. In 1981 R. J. Henle, a Jesuit at St Louis University, said flatly of Transcendental Thomism: "It is not a version of Thomism".[16] Karl Rahner said that when the Transcendental Method took over, that was "the end of Neo-Scholasticism as it had been understood since the second half of the nineteenth century".[17] Not the transformation, the end.

---

[16] Henle, "Transcendental Thomism", p. 355.
[17] Rahner, Foreword to Muck, *The Transcendental Method*, p. 10.

The end of Neo-Scholasticism

Prior to Vatican II

I said that Neo-Scholasticism triumphed for a time in the early years of the twentieth century. However, new movements, such as the biblical movement, Catholic Action, the liturgical movement and, later, the ecumenical movement, appeared in the Catholic Church and, as I will say, began to transform it.[18] There was little Thomism in the literature which circulated in these movements, which attracted gifted students, so that it was less and less talked about. Raymond Nogar, a Dominican who had been a professor of philosophy in Rome, said in 1998 that Thomism had been under attack in Europe from around 1920 and that "by 1940, Thomism as a system was dead in Europe".[19] Publication of the *Revue néo-scholastique de philosophie* had been interrupted during World War II and when it resumed in 1946 it became the *Revue philosophique de Louvain*. This was a sign.

Vatican II

At Vatican II it immediately became apparent that the bishops, and indeed all active Catholics, were divided into two opposing camps, which were called "progressive"[20] and "conservative". If the conservatives had had their way, the council would have reinstated Thomism as the thought-system of the Church. When votes were taken, however, it was found that the great majority of the world's bishops were progressive and the council, quite consciously and indeed quite loudly, did not do this. This led Gerald McCool to say that "the history of the modern Neo-Thomist movement, whose magna carta was *Aeterni Patris* [1879], reached its end at the Second Vatican Council".[21]

The present situation

The rules for the training of priests-to-be which were issued in 1970 say that their training in philosophy "must be based on that always

---

[18] See below, p. 136.
[19] Nogar, *Lord of the Absurd*, p. 63.
[20] In Catholic-Church-speak "modern" was a bad word, so a similar movement used a different word.
[21] McCool, *The Neo-Thomists*, p. 230; these are the last words of the book.

Chapter 2: *A Short History of Scholasticism*

valid philosophical patrimony whose witnesses are the great Christian philosophers" (# 71), which is not specific. The *Code of Canon Law* which was promulgated in January 1983 says: "Philosophical formation [of future priests] must be based on the philosophical heritage that is perennially valid, and it is also to take account of philosophical investigations over the course of time" (canon 251). A Thomist might say that "the philosophical heritage that is perennially valid" can only mean Thomism, but the code did not say that. In the United States surveys of philosophy departments in Catholic colleges and universities revealed that Thomism was there in decline and was going to decline further.[22] Another sign of the times is that in 1990 *The New Scholasticism* became the *American Catholic Philosophical Quarterly*.

John Paul II's encyclical *Fides et Ratio* says that "the Church has been justified in consistently proposing Saint Thomas as a master of thought" (# 43). It applauds Leo XIII's "insistence upon the incomparable value of the philosophy of Saint Thomas" (# 57) and it says that the Thomistic revival which followed produced "a powerful array of thinkers" (# 58). However, it says that it is philosophical pride "to identify one single stream with the whole of philosophy" (# 4) and that "no historical form of philosophy can legitimately claim to embrace the totality of truth, nor to be the complete explanation of the human being, of the world and of the human being's relationship with God" (# 51). It says that "the Church has no philosophy of her own nor does she canonise one particular philosophy in preference to others" (# 49). It praises Suarez (# 62) and it says that there were non-Thomists before and after 1879 who, "adopting more recent currents of thought", produced "philosophical works of great influence and lasting value" (# 59). The praise of Thomism was perhaps a eulogy at its funeral.

Catholic priests-to-be are still required to study philosophy, but whereas they used everywhere to study Scholastic Philosophy, often using the same textbooks and consulting the same authors, now what they study varies greatly.

---

[22] *American Catholic Philosophical Quarterly*, vol. 73, annual supplement.

Conclusion

Scholasticism has had three periods of dominance in the Western Catholic Church. The first period was the twelfth to the fourteenth centuries; the second period was 1500 to 1650; the third period was 1880 to 1960. These dates are approximate. Outside these periods, which is to say during about three-quarters of the time, it existed in small enclaves.

Chapter 3

A History of Personalism

"The person" is an immensely important term in Christian theology but I am going to talk here about its use in non-theological contexts.

The word "person" in the world at large: some non-personalist uses of the word

In Shakespeare, the word "person" means clothes and general appearance. In Henry IV part 1 a character says:

Thus did I keep my person fresh and new,

meaning his appearance, and another asks:

*what are thou
That counterfiet'st the person of a king?*

That is, "What are you, who are not a king but are dressed like a king?" Hamlet says of the ghost:

*If it assume my noble father's person,
I'll speak to it,*

that is, "If it is dressed like my noble father".

Later, the word "person" meant a woman who was not a lady. Sometimes it was a question of class: the *Oxford English Dictionary* quotes this from 1782: "Do you suppose a young *lady* would want to take advantage of a *person* in trade?"; and in Gilbert and Sullivan's *The Mikado* (1885), when Pooh-Bah, who is a frightful snob, is asked to let three young ladies be introduced to him, he refuses, saying, "They are not young ladies, they are young persons". At other times it was a question of morals: for instance, in Dickens's *Martin Chuzzlewit* (1843) a man arrives at a hotel with a young woman, the landlady refers to her as a "very young lady" and the censorious Mr Pecksniff severely corrects her, saying, "Person! young person!"

In legal parlance, "person" used to mean either an individual human being, or a formally constituted group of human beings with rights and duties recognised by the law and in particular with the right to own property. In 1690 John Locke said that "person" is a "forensic" or legal term.[1] In his *Commentaries on the Laws of England,* Sir William Blackstone said: "Natural persons are such as the God of nature formed us; artificial [persons] are such as are created and devised by human laws for the purposes of society and government; which are called corporations or bodies politic". Not long after that Abraham Tucker said that "a crowd is no distinct existence" but "if the same people be erected into a corporation "they become a person in law capable to sue and be sued". In 1883 the English parliament declared that "the word 'Person' shall extend to a Body Politic, Corporate or Collegiate, as well as an Individual". When the word is used in this way, a married couple can be said to be one person, which sounds obviously wrong until one realises that all that is meant is that they can jointly own property. A current *Australian Legal Dictionary* defines person in this way but it is not how the word is ordinarily used now.

In ordinary usage, the word "person" has been and is used as the singular of "people": for instance, the answer to the question, "How many people were there?" might be: "Only one person came". Sometimes "personal" means "private" as in "private life" as opposed to "public life", and then "the personal sphere" means family life, romances, affairs, hobbies and so on as opposed to the "public" activities of the state, businesses, courts and similar institutions. A politician might feel obliged to answer questions about his work, but if an interviewer were to ask him about his marriage he might say: "My personal life is my own business and I will not answer any questions about it". Buber uses the term "person" in this way in *I and Thou* and when in 1940 someone said that "the things of the world", by which he meant in particular the actions of the government, are outside the zone of ethics, Bonhoeffer said that he was restricting ethics to "the personal [i.e., the private] sphere".[2]

It used to be standard practice, in English, to use the word "man" for human beings in general but it was seen that we should not use "man" for a human being who may be male or female or for men and women taken together, so "chairman" became "chairperson" and so on. This is not precisely personalist language.

---

[1] Locke, *Essay Concerning Human Understanding,* book 2, chap. 27, # 26.
[2] Bonhoeffer, *Ethics,* p. 286.

Chapter 3: *A History of Personalism*

Finally, the Latin word *persona* was and still is sometimes used in English for the man or woman who we want to appear to be, or for what we would now call the image of himself or herself that a person wants to project. This is certainly not a personalist sense.

Christians, especially perhaps Catholics, used often to talk of souls where today we would talk of persons. They quoted Augustine's saying, "I would know God and the soul, those and nothing more"[3] and if they asked a prospective seminarian why he wanted to be a priest, they hoped that he would say: "To save souls". When people in general began to talk about persons, some priests and others said to themselves things like this: "I find myself becoming interested in my parishioners as persons and that is wrong, I should be interested only in their souls".

In this chapter I am going to talk of how the word "person" has come to be used as it is now.

"The person" in continental philosophy in the eighteenth and nineteenth centuries

Schleiermacher (1768-1834) in Germany

In the eighteenth century, deism, which is belief in a non-personal God, and pantheism, which is belief that God is everything, were fashionable and in 1799 Schleiermacher used "personalism" for theism, which is belief in a personal God. This has virtually nothing to do with later personalism, which in the first place is about human beings.

Kant (1724-1804) also in Germany

Kant made a distinction between things, which have only relative value, and persons, who have dignity or value in themselves. He said:

> Beings whose existence does not depend on our will but on nature, if they are not rational beings, have only a relative worth as means and are therefore called "things" [*Sachen*]; on the other hand, rational beings are designated "persons" [*Personen*] because their nature indicates that they are ends in themselves, i.e., things which [*read:* beings who] may not be used merely as means. Such a being is thus an object of respect.[4]

---

[3] Augustine, *Soliloquia*, I,7.
[4] Kant, *Foundations of the Metaphysics of Morals*, pp. 52-53. This is a little past halfway through the book.

This represents a step on the way to personalism.

Kierkegaard (1813-55) in Denmark

Anyone expounding the views of Kierkegaard now is likely to use personalist language because it is in that language that we today express those ideas. He himself, however, talked for the most part about the importance of the individual and the subject. There are, nevertheless, places in his writings where he talks of the person. He hated the way in which, in the Denmark of his time, almost no one dared to be different from everyone else and he said:

> No one in our day dares to be a person. The one is so afraid of "the others" that he does not dare to be an I—that is, no one dares to be an I ... and therefore becomes an impersonal something.... This has led to anonymity.[5]

For Kierkegaard, it is clear, a person is an "I", with emphasis on individuality. He himself, by the way, was an extreme non-conformist and in these journal entries he was justifying his own behaviour.

Kierkegaard also objected to the version of Hegelian Pantheism which was current among Danish Christians and he said things like this:

> Since Christianity is precisely the personal and entered into the world precisely for this very reason—to introduce "personality, being a person", to put an end to all abstractions, ambiguities, hoaxes, impersonalities, in which, according to Christianity, evil has its very home, it is readily apparent that the official proclamation of Christianity does away with Christianity.[6]

He said: "An impersonal proclamation is the abolition of Christianity",[7] and "Christianity is rooted in the view of existence which says that all salvation is related to becoming personality".[8]

In these and other passages Kierkegaard said what personalists were later to say and he used the word "person" as they did and do (except that we would say that salvation is related to being a person, not to becoming personality). He did not make "person" his central or most frequently used term and so cannot properly be called a personalist, but he was certainly a precursor of personalism and when his writ-

---

[5] Kierkegaard, *Journals and Papers*, vol. 3, p. 486. See also p. 491.
[6] Ibid., p. 487, undated entry of 1854.
[7] Ibid., p. 488, same entry.
[8] Ibid., p. 490, entry of 17 May 1855.

Chapter 3: *A History of Personalism* 51

ings became widely known in the twentieth century, personalists read them with delight.

Developments in Germany, leading to Personalism

Hermann Lotze studied and taught medicine, then switched to psychology, which at that time was a branch of philosophy so that he became a philosopher. Writing (it is said) beautiful German, he revived theism and insisted on the reality of individual selves or persons. He is also credited with being the father of value-philosophy.

William Stern, a psychologist who was also a philosopher, wrote *Person und Sache (Person and Thing)* in three volumes, published in 1906, 1918 and 1924 respectively. The subtitle of this work was *A Critical Personalism* and I mention him because he identified himself as a personalist as early as 1906. He presented a sort of pantheistic personalism, according to which all persons are elements of God, the All-Person. This is extremely unusual among personalists.

France

In his old age Charles Renouvier (1815-1903) gave his philosophy a definitive form and in 1903, the year in which he died, *Le personnalisme* was published, and when after his death in 1932 an essay and book by Lucien Laberthonnière, which had been written in the eighteen-nineties, were published, the editor gave them the titles "Première esquisse du système personnaliste" and *Esquisse d'une philosophie personnaliste.*

Personalism in England and Scotland up to World War I

In the nineteenth century, in British academic circles, Hegelian pantheism was to some extent fashionable while in the world at large there was much emphasis on scientific and technological progress. It seems that to some scholars in Oxford, who were religious or humanistic in their thinking, all this seemed terribly impersonal. In their lectures, writings and (I am sure) conversations they said that they were for *the person.* One such scholar was T. H. Green (1836-82), who had great influence in England from about 1880 to 1914 (that is, mostly after his death). In his *Prologomena to Ethics,* consisting of lectures given in the last fifteen years of his life and published in the year after his death, there was a section on "The Personal Character of the Moral Ideal" in which he defined persons as "self-conscious subjects" and also as "self-objectifying agents"; he said that persons are "agents who are ends to themselves" and that persons are "capable each of conceiving himself and the bettering of his life as an end to himself".[9] He said that there had been talk of progress, described as a divine principle realising itself in man, and he asked: "Does it realise itself in persons, in you and me, or in some impersonal Humanity", or in a nation, or in society as an organisation? In persons, he answered firmly, and said:

> There can be nothing in a nation however exalted its mission, or in a society however perfectly organised, which is not in the persons composing the nation or the society. Our ultimate standard of worth is an ideal of personal worth. To speak of any progress or improvement of a nation or a society or mankind, except as relative to some greater worth of persons, is to use words without meaning.[10]

This might sound individualistic but Green spoke positively of society, "founded on the recognition by persons of each other, as persons, i.e., as beings who are ends to themselves" and involving "some practical recognition of personality by another, of an 'I' by a 'Thou' and a 'Thou' by an 'I'." Green said that only in living mutual relationships with other persons can we really live as persons and achieve fulfilment.[11] On social issues he was a "responsible collectivist" and he has been seen as an ancestor of the British Labour Party.[12] This was personalism virtually complete, and in its own terms (except that the word "personalism" was not used and later personalists use the word "community" for what Green called "society").

James McTaggart Ellis McTaggart, to give him his long and curious name, taught at Cambridge. He was one of the last "British Idealists" who were philosophical descendants of Hegel and he wrote books which were mostly published after 1900. Several of them were about Hegel and in 1901 he published *Hegelian Cosmology*, in which he said that the Absolute comprises a community of selves. He did not call

---

[9] Four short quotations are from Green, *Prologemena to Ethics*, pp. 192-199.
[10] Ibid., p. 193.
[11] Three short quotations, ibid., pp. 199-200.
[12] Quinton, *Thoughts and Thinkers*, p. 194.

himself a personalist but Knudson says that he was an atheistic personalist, which is unusual. In 1902 eight Oxford scholars, including H. Rashdall, produced *Personal Idealism,* in which, obviously, they combined talk of the person with the subjectivism that had been current in England. I have headed this section "Personalism in England and Scotland" but the movement did not have that name and was not fully developed.

When around 1900 some philosophers appeared in England who wanted to make philosophy into a science,[13] the field of philosophy became the battleground of a war between them and more traditional arts-faculty philosophers. The scientifically-minded philosophers won and personalism and value-theory almost vanished from university philosophy departments in the United Kingdom and subsequently in the rest of the English-speaking world.

Personalism in the United States
Before Borden Parker Bowne

Walt Whitman, the poet, who died in 1892, had a strong belief in the worth of individual men and women and he proposed what Arthur E. Briggs calls a "personalist religion".[14] As an American, he was strongly in favour of democracy and he said that the country was founded on "the all-levelling aggregate of democracy", but he insisted on the "individual personal dignity of a single person, either male or female" and maintained that the country stood on "a lofty and hitherto unocccupied framework or platform of personalism".[15]

New England Transcendentalism flourished from around 1830 to 1850 and it was embodied in a Transcendental Club which Emerson founded in 1836. It was different from Unitarianism and Calvinism, both of which existed in New England, and it was intellectually vague but emotionally uplifting. The club was a quasi-church and

---

[13] See above, p. 20.
[14] Briggs, *Walt Whitman Thinker and Artist*, pp. 96-98. Briggs says: "It is in Whitman's personalistic humanism that one will find the synthetic principle which harmonises sex, science, religion and government without sacrifice of man or men" (p. 15).
[15] Whitman wrote "Democray" and "Personalism" and then combined them in *Democratic Vistas*. The quotations are from "Personalism".

its ideas would probably now be called a spirituality. Bronson Alcott (1799-1888), a New Englander, had some revolutionary ideas about education, established schools for poor children in the south, became known, was drawn into the Transcendental group and became a roving promoter of its ideas. He knew Whitman and after 1868 he used the term "personalism" to define his own philosophy, in so far as it could be defined.

George Holmes Howison (1834-1916, at Berkeley from 1884) was a pantheistic idealist but in 1892-93 he moved away from pantheism while remaining an idealist and asserted the reality of individual human persons. He called his system "personal idealism". In 1907 Mary Whitton Calkins called herself an "absolutistic personalist".

Borden Parker Bowne and Boston Personalism

The most significant figure in the history of personalism in the United States was Borden Parker Bowne. Born in 1847, he was a Methodist and he was ordained as a deacon in 1872. In 1873-75 he was a postgraduate philosophy student in Germany, where he was influenced by Lotze, and in France. In 1876 he began teaching philosophy in Boston University, which was Methodist, and he wrote a number of important books, including *Metaphysics* (1882, revised edition 1898). He also campaigned for various causes, including votes for women. In his earlier books he did not make much use of the term "person" but towards the end of his life he began to call himself a Personalist and in 1908 he published *Personalism*. He died in 1910.

Edgar Sheffield Brightman was born in 1884. After graduating elsewhere, he studied under Bowne in Boston in 1910 and he was ordained a Methodist deacon in that year. He was in Germany for the academic year 1910-11 and then taught in the United States, not in Boston. In 1919 he became the Borden Parker Bowne professor of philosophy in Boston University, where he taught until his death in 1953. He was a Personalist and was inspired by Bowne.

Various men who had studied at Boston carried Personalism to other centres in the United States. One, Ralph Tyler Flewelling (1871-1960), carried it to the University of Southern California, where in 1920 he launched *The Personalist,* a quarterly. In its early issues it was openly religious, with reviews of books about the Bible and other religious

matters. Its first issue had an article by the editor, "Can Civilisation Become Christian?", and an article in 1924 said:
> Personalism is a defender, in philosophy, of human courage. It magnifies insight, faces human facts with understanding, sustains self-respect, and, in general, carries the foundations and encouragements of Christian faith into philosophical inquiry.[16]

The Personalist was also literary, with poetry and with articles about novelists and poets. It had many articles about Borden Parker Bowne, but the writers clearly wanted to move forward—in "Tasks Confronting a Personalist Philosophy" (1921) Brightman said: "Bowne must not be erected into the St Thomas of Methodism".[17] Later, there were so many Personalists in California that it became possible to talk of the California Personalist Tradition.

Personalist ideas

Personalism in general

Personalism is a philosophy which gets its name from its principal theme and indeed from the use of the word "person". It was from the first an agent-philosophy, not a spectator-philosophy.[18] Bowne said: "Not to form abstract theories but to formulate and understand this personal life of ours is the first and last duty of philosophy".[19] He also said:
> Our first step towards the personal interpretation of experience consists in the insight that we are in a personal world from the start, and that the first, last and only duty of philosophy is to interpret this world of personal life and relations.[20]

This meant that values were of prime importance to personalists, and when in 1875 *The Personalist Forum* was launched its editor said in the first issue that Personalism is philosophy done with the belief that people matter, which is a value judgement.

The Personalists believed in souls and spiritual realities and so were opposed to materialism, which in its physico-chemical form reduced

---

[16] Beardslee, "Personalism and Behaviour", p. 12.
[17] Brightman, "Tasks Confronting a Personalist Philosophy", pp. 164-165.
[18] See above, p. 18.
[19] Bowne, *Personalism*, p. 75.
[20] Ibid., p. 53.

human beings to elementary particles so that the person disappeared. Personalists believed in spiritual realities such as the soul, so that Personalism was what I have called a "high" philosophy.

Only an individual, not a species, says "I", and "Thou" can be said only to an individual. Personalists, therefore, believed in the value of individuals and were opposed to materialists who regarded human beings as just another animal species and who said that what mattered was the species, not any individuals, that is, not persons. There was perhaps a tendency at first to be individualistic but, as we shall see, it became characteristic of Personalists to insist on the value of relationships with other persons.

Belief in free will was an essential element of Personalism and it was often included in definitions of the person.

Also, virtually all Personalists believed and believe in a personal God. In England and Scotland they were non-Catholic Christians, on the continent of Europe they were mostly Catholics and, as we have seen, the original Boston Personalists were Methodists.

Boston Personalism

When Bowne studied in Germany and France in 1873-75, the influence of Kant and Hegel was still strong and subjectivism was dominant in philosophy faculties. Bowne and his followers seem to have accepted this, as far as the material world was concerned: in 1927 Knudson talked of a realistic personalism, which affirmed "the extramental existence of the material world", but he said that this had been disappearing because of "the criticism to which has been subjected by modern idealism", leaving idealistic Personalism in possession of the field, and he included subjectivism in his definition of Personalism. That is, Boston Personalism is subjectivistic.

Bowne, however, did not teach that there exists only a universal Mind in which everything we know, ourselves included, is a thought.[21] Knudson says: "The belief in the real existence of individual minds or persons or souls or selves underlies all the different forms of personalism", and makes it different from absolute subjectivism; in opposition to Hegel, he says, "all personalists hold that the self has a unique and distinct character of its own".[22]

[21] Bowne, *Metaphysics*, 1st edition, p. 452.
[22] Knudson, *The Philosophy of Personalism*, p. 68.

In accord with their views of matter and the human person, many Boston Personalists said that a human person *is* his or her soul or mind and *has* a body. This conception tended to remove the body and material considerations from the personal realm and to make Personalism a one-sidedly spiritual philosophy.

Finally, while most (perhaps all) Personalists insisted that a human being can attain fulfilment as a person only through communication and a sharing of life with other persons, and while they attached great importance to small communities so formed, they may have tended to be hostile towards large societies, which are necessarily somewhat impersonal. Thus Personalism may have appealed to refined and privileged people who lacked concern for the world at large. At least some authors in the movement saw this tendency and opposed it. The first issue of *The Personalist* had an article by its editor, Flewelling, in which he spoke of Personalists' "previous devotion to individualistic theories" and he went on: "May not the culture of individualism found in the end to wreck itself by its principle of selfishness give way to the higher culture of personalism?" Personalists, he said, had been individualistic but they were "seeing with new vision that no elements are cultural unless they include the well-being of all" and "if the world is to move forward to a better day it can only be by an advance from selfish individualism towards an altruism which brings the highest development of personality". [23]

Twentieth-Century Personalism in Germany and France

In Germany, Max Scheler

Born in Munich in 1874 of a Protestant father and a Jewish mother, Max Scheler was brought up as a Jew but became a Catholic at fourteen. At nineteen, on a summer holiday in Austria, he met a married woman, Amelie von Dewitz, who lived in Berlin. In the autumn he enrolled in the medical faculty in Munich but, instead of studying, engaged in "frantic debauchery". In 1894 he transferred to Berlin, switched to philosophy and had an affair with Amelie. Within about a year she and her husband were divorced, she and Scheler married, and he adopted her daughter. He left the Catholic Church then. In

---

[23] Flewelling, "Can Civilisation Become Christian?", p. 15.

1895 they went to Jena, where they lived for ten years, during which Scheler wrote his doctoral dissertation and became a lecturer. In 1900 they had a son. Scheler's thesis director was Rudolf Eucken, who was what I have called a high philosopher. He was also an engaged philosopher, as opposed to a detached observer and commentator; he travelled widely and talked about social and cultural problems to such an extent that he was later given a Nobel Peace Prize. Scheler greatly admired him for this. On the other hand, Eucken was a kind of subjectivist and this troubled Scheler. In 1901 Scheler met Husserl (who was fifteen years older than he and like him partly Jewish), read Bergson (also a half-Jewish philosopher), and, parting philosophically from Eucken, he became a phenomenologist.

In 1907, because Amelie was jealous of a woman or women in Jena, the couple moved to Munich, where Scheler lectured in ethics and psychology. In 1908 he fell in love with a student, Maerit Furtwaengler, and after a difficult year he and Amelie separated. She told a newspaper that he was in debt because of his affairs and that his wife and children lived in poverty. He sued the paper for printing this, the paper produced evidence of his immoral behaviour and in April 1910 he was not only dismissed from the university of Munich but forbidden by law to teach in any German university. So in the summer of 1910 he was, at the age of thirty-six, out of work and separated from his wife, his ten-year-old son and his adopted daughter.

He moved to Göttingen, where Husserl was lecturing at the university. He stayed there with his friend Dietrich von Hildebrand and joined a group of phenomenologists. He wrote and he also became a freelance lecturer who could hold the attention of an audience for hours by the sheer force of his personality, so that for the phenomenologists he became their star. In 1912 he and Amelie were divorced and he moved back to Munich, where he married Maerit in the Catholic Church (he was 38, she was 21; in the eyes of the Church his marriage to Amelie was invalid). In 1912 his book *Ressentiment* was published and it was followed in 1913 by a book on love (*The Nature of Sympathy*). Things were looking up.

In 1914 World War I began and in 1915 Scheler was re-converted to Catholicism. For the next five or six years, his "Catholic years" during which he was in his early forties, he was a leading Catholic

Chapter 3: *A History of Personalism* 59

intellectual who wrote many articles and gave many speeches to Catholic audiences. During this time he talked of "the person" and in 1916 he published a large work the subtitle of which was *A New Attempt Towards the Foundation of an Ethical Personalism*,[24] and in his lectures he talked of personal culture and of how education should form the whole person.[25] He also gave partiotic speeches about the bad influence of capitalist England.

After the war a new university in Cologne, Catholic in inspiration and attended by seminarians and other Catholics, gave him a teaching position and he also gave lectures to large audiences all over Germany, telling people, especially Catholics, to join in the rebuilding of Germany. He became internationally famous.

Around 1921, he met Maria Scheu, a student, and they became lovers. In March 1923 his wife Maerit left him, they were divorced, and in April 1924 he married Maria in a civil marriage but according to Staude he continued to see Maerit and he told her that she was his true love. The break-up of his marriage and the civil remarriage which followed it were too much for the Catholic authorities in Cologne, who told the seminarians and other Catholic students not to take his ethics courses. He left the Church, which he began to attack, and he also ceased to believe in a personal God.[26] In 1928 he had a stroke and six days later he died, aged fifty-four. The speaker at his grave said: "The concept of person is given a fundamental role in Scheler's philosophy".[27] In other words, he was a Personalist.

From Germany to France

In the nineteen-twenties, perhaps because of Scheler, there was much talk of the person. Gurvitch gave a course of lectures in the Sorbonne, on contemporary German philosophy, and they were later published; of course, he talked about Scheler.

---

[24] The main title is *Formalism in Ethics and Non-Formal Ethics of Values*. An English translation was published in 1973.
[25] See Staude, *Max Scheler*, p. 251.
[26] In a book published in 1928 Scheler said: "We deny the basic presupposition of theism: a spiritual, personal God, omnipotent in his spirituality" (*Man's Place in Nature*, p. 207).
[27] Staude, *Max Scheler*, p. 251.

Nicholas Berdyaev (1874-1948) was an upper-class Russian whose mother was half French and in whose family French was the principal language. In the eighteen-nineties he became a Marxist, he engaged in some revolutionary activity and as a result he was dismissed from the university and exiled to a remote area of Russia. He switched from Marxism to subjectivism and then became an ardent Russian-Orthodox Christian, which he remained. After the 1917 revolution he returned to Moscow and founded a Free Academy of Spiritual Culture in which public lectures were given. This did not last and in 1922 he was expelled again. This time he went to Berlin, where he read Scheler's works and met Scheler. He says of him:

> He was brilliant in conversation and his thinking revealed a rich intellectual imagination. His spontaneous, gentle and almost child-like manner went hand in hand with an astonishing and rather shameless egocentricity. It was impossible to touch on any subject without his reverting to his own person, to his books and his role in life. In my opinion he was the most talented and original German philosopher of the day.[28]

Perhaps from Scheler, Berdyaev took the idea of the person and he used it, though he did not identify himself as a personalist. In 1924 he went to Paris, where of course he was quite at home.

Mounier's Personalism in France to World War II

In 1903, in Paris, Jacques Maritain (1882-1973) and his Russian-born Jewish wife Raïssa became Catholics. He studied Thomas Aquinas and became a dyed-in-the-wool Thomist. Because of the Russian connection he may have met Berdyaev and heard him talking about the person. Be that as it may, some personalist ideas entered his mind and in 1925 he published *Three Reformers,* in which he used a distinction between individual and person to make statements about the value of human beings *as persons*. In the late nineteen-twenties he and Raïssa regularly received in their house a group of interesting people. Most of them were Catholics but there were also others, including Berdyaev, who later said that "it needed a strong digestion and even stronger breathing capacities to take the large and suffocating doses of scholasticism dished up on these occasions".[29] One of the group was Emmanuel

---
[28] Berdyaev, *Dream and Reality*, p. 248.
[29] Ibid., p. 262.

Chapter 3: *A History of Personalism* 61

Mounier, a Catholic who was born in 1905 and so was about twenty-three years younger than Maritain. In 1927 he went from Grenoble to Paris for post-graduate studies in philosophy. During the winter of 1928-29 he read Péguy, who before his death in World War I had been an ardent Catholic, a socialist, the editor of a periodical and, it seemed to Mounier, the model of an engaged thinker and writer. When the world-wide depression began in 1929, some of the group judged that the existing capitalist order of Western civilisation was ending; it would be replaced, they thought, by a new order, just as at the Renaissance a new order replaced the medieval social and economic system, and they talked about what this new order should be. In 1932 they decided to launch a monthly review, to be called *Esprit*, to publicise their ideas, one of which was that the spiritual element in human life should be emphasised. Inspired by Péguy, Mounier gave up the idea of becoming an academic, with a secure income but limited freedom, abandoned his studies, and agreed to be the editor. Maritain encouraged the members of this group in its early years and he helped them financially when they launched *Esprit*, but as time went on their ideas developed while his (it seems to me) remained the same. He did not attack them by name but he was critical of them and he drops out of the history of Mounier's Personalism, with which I am concerned here.[30]

Paul Louis Landsberg was born in Germany in 1901 and he became a student and friend of Scheler. In 1926, when Scheler was still alive, Landsberg became a professor of philosophy. Because he was a Jew and hostile to Nazism, when the Nazis came to power in 1933 he left the country. He went first to France and then in 1934 to Barcelona, where he became a professor of philosophy. He associated with the *Esprit* people and when in 1934 they met to discuss their ideas, Landsberg is said to have dominated the meetings, at which he expounded Scheler's ideas, which were not the same as Maritain's but would not have been completely new to the members of the group. Their thinking now crystallised around the idea of *the person* rather than around that of *spirit* and they adopted "Personalism" as the name of their philosophy, though they did not change the name of their

[30] For more about Maritain, see below p. 78.

periodical. December 1934 is sometimes given as the birth-date of Mounier's Personalism.

Buber's *I and Thou,* published in German in 1923, was perhaps not widely known in Paris but the idea of *the other subject* was current. Mounier saw the significance of it and incorporated it into his Personalism, which from the start was not a philosophy of a solitary *I* facing an impersonal world but a philosophy of persons facing *each other* as well as the impersonal world. In 1934-35 he wrote two important articles, "Revolution personnaliste" and "Revolution communautaire" and the book *Revolution personnaliste et communautaire,* which contained these and other articles. (He said that, strictly speaking, the expression "personalist and communitarian revolution" was redundant because "communitarian" was included in "personalist".) He was opposed to both fascist and communist collectivisms, in which the individual counts for nothing except as a part of a whole, and also to capitalist individualism. In fact, Mounier regarded individualism as both the very antithesis of Personalism and its "nearest adversary", by which he meant the thing with which Personalism was most likely to be confused and against which Personalists needed most of all to be on guard. He was incensed when people who acted individualistically claimed to be personalists and he would have been appalled by people who claimed that because they were persons they had a right always to do their own thing.

At an early stage, Mounier and a certain Georges Izard became friends and associates. Izard had a group which aimed to become a political party, but Mounier seems to have wanted to keep a certain distance from party politics and in July 1933 he and Izard jointly announced their separation.

In 1933 Mounier took a teaching job in Brussels, which made editing *Esprit* in Paris difficult. In Brussels he met and in July 1935 he married a Belgian teacher, Paulette Leclerc. While on this subject I will say that they had a daughter in 1938 who unfortunately died in 1939. In that year they moved to Paris. Now let us return to 1936.

That year was a turning-point in European history. Moscow had forbidden Communist parties to join with democratic-socialist parties but after the Nazis obtained power in Germany this prohibition was cancelled and in Spain and France Communists and socialists united

Chapter 3: *A History of Personalism*   63

in "popular fronts" which won elections, in Spain in February and in France in May. In October Mounier published *Manifeste au service du personnalisme (Personalist Manifesto)*, which aimed to influence the Popular Front government. In Spain, the civil war began and Landsberg moved to France, where he became more closely associated with Mounier and wrote for *Esprit*.

I will not here attempt to follow Mounier and the *Esprit* group through the thirties, discussing their attitude towards Nazism, the Popular Front, the Spanish civil war and the Abyssinian war. I will merely say that they attracted to non-communist liberal positions many people who were not themselves "workers" and who might otherwise have found themselves on the political right.

Mounier's Personalism in Poland and the United States

The influence of Mounier and *Esprit* reached some Catholics in other countries, one of which was Poland. Many Catholics there, especially some in university circles, followed developments in France, read *Esprit* and Mounier's books, and became Personalists. One of them, Jerzy Turowicz, attended the *Esprit* congress held in France in the summer of 1939, where he met Mounier and other leaders of the movement, and he returned to Poland as a member of "the *Esprit* family".

In New York, when Dorothy Day launched *The Catholic Worker* on 1 May 1933 and the *Catholic Worker* movement came into being, she was dependent for many of her ideas on Peter Maurin, a Frenchman in his mid-fifties who had left France in 1909 but who knew of Mounier, was a reader of *Esprit* and in due course professed Personalism. The *Catholic Worker* movement thus became, quite professedly, Personalist. Also, in 1938 the editors of *Commonweal* said that their Catholic magazine was "Personalist", and they meant in Mounier's, not the Boston, way. Mounier himself said that *Commonweal* was an American *Esprit*. These magazines, and probably others, spread the word about Personalism among Catholics, not so much in clerical-academic circles as in groups which were concerned about social-justice issues.

Differences between Boston Personalism and Mounier's Personalism

As far as I know, in the thirties Mounier and his friends were unaware of Boston Personalism and the Boston Personalists were unaware of them. For one thing, they wrote in different languages on opposite sides of the Atlantic Ocean. For another, Mounier and his friends were mostly Catholics whereas Boston Personalists were predominantly Methodists. Moreover, the Boston Personalists were academics whereas Mounier was not, and *The Personalist* was a scholarly quarterly whereas *Esprit* was a monthly which dealt with current affairs, including political issues. This, incidentally, is why even now the only Personalism known to many academic philosophers in the English-speaking world is the Boston variety.

The main difference between the two Personalisms was this: Boston Personalism was subjectivistic whereas Mounier was a realist. Thus, whereas Boston Personalists said that the person is the soul or the mind, for Mounier and his followers the person was the whole human being, body and senses as well as the soul or mind; and whereas Boston Personalists tended to exclude material beings from the properly personal sphere, Mounier Personalists included them in it.

Moreover, while we have seen that in 1920 the American Personalist Flewelling rejected individualism, Mounier rejected it even more emphatically and his Personalism was more communitarian than the Boston variety.

Mounier's Personalism in the Catholic Church prior to World War II

Before World War II the Catholic Church's intellectual world was almost entirely populated by priests and priests-to-be. Dominated by Scholastic, usually Thomist, philosophers and theologians, it was not a personalist world. Also, before World War II there was often a distinctive "Catholic line" on public issues. During the Spanish civil war, for instance, in many countries the secular newspapers were hostile to Franco but Catholic periodicals attributed this to anti-Catholic prejudice and supported him. They were also pro-Salazar, when he was not in general favour. *Esprit* did not follow the Catholic line on these

Chapter 3: *A History of Personalism* 65

and other issues, so that while it showed some Catholics that it was possible to be anti-Franco without being pro-Communist, to many Catholics it seemed to be uncatholic (if I may coin a word) and in 1936, when the Spanish civil war began, it was rumoured that *Esprit*, and with it Mounier and his Personalism, were going to be condemned by the Church. Fortunately, this did not happen.

In the United States, there were perhaps two additional reasons for the non-acceptance of Personalism by the official Church and its schools. First, the association of early Personalism with Methodism and subjectivism caused many leading Catholics to distrust it. Second, American Protestants had for a long time maintained that America was in fact if not in name a Protestant country in which the Catholic Church was a foreign body, and in the nineteen-thirties many liberal American Catholics were fighting this and maintaining that Catholicism and Americanism were compatible. Since at that time Americanism entailed capitalism and competition, these Catholics stressed the Church's belief in private property and its opposition to socialism. William D. Miller says that for them "the personalist idea could only seem un-American and anti-Catholic".[31]

In my account of the development of Personalism I mentioned Scheler in Germany between 1916 and 1921, Mounier in France, Jerzy Turowicz in Poland and Dorothy Day and the *Commonweal* group in the United States. These were laypeople, to whom the inhabitants of the clerical academic world paid little attention and throughout the thirties more and more Catholic laypeople discovered Personalism or were influenced by it.

Mounier's and Polish Personalism during World War II

World War II began in September 1939, in 1940 France was invaded by Germany and it surrendered. The northern parts, which included Paris, were under German rule but the rest of the country had a French government which, centred at Vichy, set out to be different from the pre-war governments. For instance, they had been anti-clerical and it was pro-clerical. At first the publication of *Esprit* was permitted and Mounier entertained the hope that the new France might embody at

---

[31] Miller, *A Harsh and Dreadful Love*, p. 89.

least some Personalist ideals. As time went on, however, the men of Vichy became more and more rightist and pro-Nazi. They showed both these things by persecuting Jews. Mounier soon distanced himself from them, *Esprit* was forbidden and there could be no more *Esprit* conferences. In April 1941 the Mouniers had a second daughter and in January 1942 he was arrested on suspicion of doing resistance work, imprisoned for about ten months, then released. He spent the rest of the war hiding with his wife and child in an out-of-the-way village in the Italian zone. During this time he wrote a long book, *Traité du caractère (The Character of Man)*, and *L'affrontement chrétien (The Spoil of the Violent)*. Landsberg was arrested in March 1943 and taken to the concentration camp in Oranienberg, where in April 1944 he died.

In Poland, after 1941, when it was entirely occupied by Germany, Personalism went underground.

Personalism in the Catholic Church during World War II

In France, during the occupation the official Catholic Church at least seemed, in general, not merely to accept but to be in favour of the Vichy government. Once more, Mounier disagreed with "the Catholic line", with the result that when he was imprisoned in 1942 the chaplain refused to give him communion. However, Personalist influence can be seen in Pius XII's Christmas message of 1942, in which he said: "The origin and the primary scope of social life is the conservation, development and perfection of the human person",[32] and in a passage from his encyclical on the Mystical Body of Christ which I shall quote later.[33] Someone in the team which wrote those documents was a Personalist.

---

[32] The implementation by the Nazis of the Final Solution, with mass deportations and killings of Jews, began in March 1942. Pius XII was informed of this and was asked to condemn it. In his message of 24 December 1942, quoted above, he spoke of "hundreds of thousands" who "sometimes only by reason of their nationality or race" were being killed. He has been praised by people who say that he was clearly condemning what is now called the Holocaust, and he has been blamed by others for talking only in general terms.

[33] See below, p. 191.

Chapter 3: *A History of Personalism* 67

In French Canada, in 1943 Charles de Koninck wrote a violent attack on Personalism. He named no Personalists, showed that he thought that Personalism was a form of egoism, said that the sin of the angels was personalistic,[34] said that Personalism was a speculatively feeble form of Pelagianism and, quoting Marx and Stalin, linked it to Communism. In an even more violent preface to this book, the Cardinal Archbishop of Quebec said that Personalism had become fashionable but, he said, we do not need a Personalist conception of marriage or a Christian and socialist Personalism.[35] I suspect that these men, whose language was French, were strongly influenced by what was going on in France.

Personalism immediately after World War II

When in 1944 France was liberated, Mounier became celebrated as a thinker, a man of integrity and to some extent a hero. He preached Personalism with all his might and produced two more books, *Qu'est-ce que le personnalisme?* (1947) and *Le personnalisme* (1949), with the result that soon everyone was talking about Personalism, Existentialism and Marxism, and like Marxism it was not only a philosophy but a dynamic movement.[36] Also, when the *Mouvement républicain populaire,* a Christian-Democratic political party, was formed in November 1944, many of the people in it had been influenced by Personalism in their formative years. Mounier himself, however, again kept his distance from party politics.

For some years, Mounier was more opposed to capitalism than to Communism, and to America more than to Russia. Yet again he disagreed with most Catholics. In Poland, the Germans were driven out but the Poles found themselves with a Communist government. Probably thanks to Mounier's anti-americanism, the Personalists enjoyed considerable freedom. Jerzy Turowicz launched a weekly, *Tygodnik Powszechny,* and a year later a monthly, *Znak.* In May 1946 Mounier visited Poland, met Turowicz again, gave an address at the

---

[34] *"Le péché des anges fut une erreur pratiquement personnaliste"* (de Koninck, *De la primauté du bien commun contre les personnalistes [The Primacy of the Common Good, Against Personalists],* p.3).
[35] Ibid. p. xviii.

Jagellonian University in Warsaw and undoubtedly talked for hours with Turowicz and his friends.

Mounier and Paulette had a third daughter in 1947 and I am sure that he was delighted to see how almost all over the world the word "person" was more and more used. For instance, in 1948 the United Nations issued a Declaration of Human Rights in which there was talk of "the dignity and worth of the human person". Then in March 1950, at the age of forty-five, Mounier had a heart attack and died. If books are any indication, the movement flowed on: in 1951 Jean Lacroix published *Marxisme, existentialisme, personnalisme,* on the three philosophies which were discussed in post-war France, Landsberg's *Problèmes du personnalisme* was published posthumously in 1952, and there were many other books besides these.

Personalism and Existentalism

After World War II, Jean-Paul Sartre, who wrote not only long and short philosophical books but also novels, plays, films and a song, became an international celebrity and his kind of Existentialism became fashionable everywhere. Both Personalism and Existentialism are concerned with finding a meaning in life and not in the first place with ultimate causes or with language, so that there is a resemblance between them because of which Scholastic and analytical philosophers often lump them together. Neither, however, is an offshoot of the other: Personalism has almost always been theistic whereas Existentialism has been predominantly (not exclusively) atheistic; Personalism affirms objective values, as Existentialism generally does not; and Sartrean Existentialism was individualistic, which Personalism was not. Personalism, therefore, should not be classed as a form of Existentialism and in Paris after World War II the Personalists and the Existentialists were separate groups.

---

[36] See Kelly, *Pioneer of the Catholic Revival*, p. 143.

Personalism in the English-speaking world after World War II

In philosophy departments of universities

Boston Personalism has had a continuous if somewhat marginal existence in universities in the United States.[37] The main philosophical association there used to be dominated by analytical philosophers and I suspect that they despised but tolerated the Personalists, who since 1938 have met on their own as a Personalistic Discussion Group. *The Personalist Forum,* a bi-annual publication, was launched in 1985 to replace *The Personalist,* which had ceased publication in 1979. It is published at Furman University, Greenville, Ohio, and in its first issue the editor said:

> Our aim is not simply to perpetuate the tradition of Boston personalism. We plan to draw on personalism in other traditions, East and West, including Max Scheler and Thomas Masaryk, Emmanuel Mounier and Karol Wojtyla, Nakamura Hajime and Watsuji Tetsuro.[38]

In the Fall issue of 1988 it commemorated fifty years of the Personalistic Discussion group. In September 1991 a Conference on Persons was held at Mansfield College, Oxford, UK; it was attended by seventy-five scholars from Europe, the United States and Canada and its proceedings were published in *The Personalist Forum,* which had sponsored it. In 1995, *Metaphysical Personalism,* which is by Charles Conti and about Austin Farrer, was published by the Oxford University Press. Also, Leon D. Stitskin, the professor of Jewish Philosophy at Yeshiva University in New York, maintains that Jewish philosophy is personalist.[39] Finally, a conference on Christian Philosophy was held in the Franciscan University of Steubenville in November 2000 on the subject of "Christian Personalism".

---

[37] Surveys of Boston Personalism have appeared, one being *The Philosophy of Personalism* (1927) by Knudson, who had been a student of Bowne's. A more recent book is *The Boston Personalist Tradition in Philosophy, Social Ethics, and Theology,* edited by Deats and Robb (1986).

[38] *The Personalist Forum,* vol.1, no. 1, Spring 1985, p. 4.

[39] See Stitskin, *Jewish Philosophy: A Study in Personalism* and *Eight Jewish Philosophers in the Tradition of Personalism.*

However, when the philosophy departments in secular universities in the English-speaking world were taken over by scientifically-minded philosophers, who established a tradition, Personalism almost disappeared from this large part of the philosophical scene and this is why many American and English encyclopedias and dictionaries of philosophy, in their entries for "personalism", deal only or mainly with Boston Personalism and are dismissive of it. For instance, the 1968 edition of the *Encyclopedia Americana* says that Personalistic Idealism, which involves the idea that belief in matter or non-mental being is unreasonable, has been regarded as typical personalism. A *Dictionary of Philosophy* (Pan Books, 1979) says that personalism is "largely of twentieth-century American origin" and that it is "Idealist in character". The *Routledge Encyclopedia of Philosophy* (1998) begins by saying, "Personalism is the thesis that only persons (self-conscious agents) and their states and characteristics exist", says later that "for the personalist, persons are simple (non-composite)" and it ends with the words: "See Idealism". The *New Fontana Dictionary of Modern Thought* (1999) says that personalism is

> a form of Idealism which holds that everything real is a person or an element in the existence of some person... . The personal idealism of such dissenters from absolute idealism as McTaggart and Rashdall around the turn of the century is perhaps the most philosophically significant form of personalism, but it has been more recently exemplified in modern French Neo-Thomism, and there has been a continuing tradition of personalism in the USA with a strong theistic tendency (see Theism).[40]

The Cambridge Dictionary of Philosophy (1995) says that personalism was "a version of personal idealism that flourished in the United States (principally at Boston University) from the late nineteenth to the mid-twentieth century", and goes on at length about this; then it adds:

> Another version of personalism developed in France out of the Neo-Scholastic tradition. E. Mounier (1905-1950), J. Maritain (1882-1972), and E. Gilson (1884-1978) identified themselves as personalists, inasmuch as they viewed the infinite person (God) and finite persons as the source and locus of intrinsic value.

[40] This is in the third edition, revised, of the *Fontana Dictionary of Modern Thought*, edited by Alan Bullock and Stephen Trombley, first published in 1977. Concerning McTaggart and Rashdall, see above, p. 43.

Chapter 3: *A History of Personalism* 71

This implies that anyone who believes in a personal God is a personalist and that the men whom it mentions believed in one "infinite person (God)", not three divine persons. However, at least Mounier got a mention. Thomas Mautner, in *A Dictionary of Philosophy* (Oxford, 1996) says that personalism is "a view which emphasises the importance of personhood" and he says that it is, first, the Boston tradition in the United States and, second, "the thought of Emmanuel Mounier (1905-1950) and the philosophical movement which it has inspired". This is better.

A quite extraordinary account of Personalism is to be found in *The Oxford Dictionary of Philosophy* (1994), according to which it is this:

> The philosophy of probability pioneered by Ramsey and de Finetti, and furthered by American statistician L. J. Savage in his *Foundations of Statistics* (1954). Personalism rejects the view that probabilities are "out there" waiting to be discovered. It views assignments of probability to events as purely personal expressions of the degree of confidence to be had in the occurrence of the event.

It goes on like this for twenty lines, then says:

> In an older usage, personalism is the theistic stress on the existence of divine personality, or any philosophy according to which the individual thinker is the starting-point of theory.

I regret to have to say that Frederick Copleston failed to appreciate Personalism. In 1956 he published *Contemporary Philosophy: Studies of Logical Positivism and Existentialism*, the second part of which was about "continental personalist and existentialist philosophies". He had about twenty pages on personalism, which included five pages on Mounier in which he said that that personalism was not a form of existentialism,[41] and about a hundred on existentialism. In his *History of Philosophy* he talked about "Personal Idealism" in Britain and the United States[42] and he had a few pages about Mounier,[43] but personalism does not figure in his *History* as a significant movement. In *Religion and Philosophy* he did not discuss it and in the essay "Modern Philosophy and Religion" he discussed Sartre and Jaspers, not Buber, Scheler nor Mounier. That is, he was not ignorant of Personalism but

---

[41] Copleston, *Contemporary Philosophy*, pp. 103-124.
[42] Copleston, *History of Philosophy*, vol. 8, pp. 237-253, 289-303.
[43] Ibid., vol. 9, pp. 310-317.

he seems to have been unaware of its immense influence on contemporary religion—Buber, Scheler and Mounier, for instance, have had far more influence on religion than Sartre or Jaspers.

Psychologists

Most psychologists in the twentieth century, especially in its early years, wanted to be accepted as scientists and so avoided unscientific terms like "person". In the *Penguin Dictionary of Psychology* (1985), Arthur S. Reher felt that he had to include an entry for "person" and disdainfully defined it as follows:

> *Person:* Psychology, in one guise or another, concerns itself with entities that behave, act, think, emote and do so within the context of some social and physical environment. When such an entity is a member of the species *Homo sapiens* the term *person* is appropriately used as a label.

Behaviorism, which was madly scientific, became dominant in many psychology faculties. This proved unsatisfactory to some clinical psychologists, so that Existential and Humanistic Psychology appeared on the scene. In 1951 Carl Rogers wrote *Client-Centred Therapy* and went on to talk also about "student-centred teaching". He then began to call his approach "person-centred" and wrote *On Becoming a Person: A Therapist's View of Psychotherapy* (1961), *Person to Person* (1967) and later "The Foundations of the Person-Centred Approach" (1981). He had become a personalist, whether he knew it or not.

The wider English-speaking world

The word "person" has been used constantly and there were some individual figures who, while they did not identify themselves as Personalists, talked a great deal about the person and had a great influence. Among these was John Macmurray, who wrote *The Self as Agent* (1957) and *Persons in Relation* (1961).

In the general public, one finds that everyone is talking about the person now, in a personalist way, so that the writer of a television drama can give a character the line, "I'm a person, I must be treated with respect!" and know that viewers will not only understand this but feel that it is obviously true. Personalism may not be fashionable in the philosophy departments of our universities but it has become an

Chapter 3: *A History of Personalism* 73

important element of Western culture, and indeed of contemporary international culture. If ever the ideas of feminism or environmentalism become generally accepted, so that almost everyone takes them for granted, these movements will cease to exist, and to a large extent this has happened with Personalism.

Personalism in the Catholic Church
Immediately after World War II
When World War II ended, the movements which I mentioned earlier—in particular, the biblical, liturgical and ecumenical movements—gathered momentum in the Catholic Church so that one could see it changing. I said earlier that, generally speaking, the people in these movements were not inspired by Thomism. I cannot maintain that they all professed Personalism. However, there was much that was Personalistic about them, as will later appear.[44]

When conservatives in positions of authority saw that seminarians, young priests and young religious seemed to have a new culture and were saying, for instance, that Catholic institutions should be less authoritarian, and when they judged that this was happening because of new lecturers who were talking about "the person", they complained about the destructive influence of Personalism and sometimes had those lecturers removed. At other times these conservatives had not heard of Personalism but they had heard of Existentialism, which was being talked about everywhere at that time, and they thought that they saw it spreading in the Church, doing harm. But the movements could not be stopped.

Lublin Personalism and Karol Wojtyla[45]
The Personalism of Mounier, which had existed in Poland before World War II and resurfaced after it, existed mainly in Catholic university circles. Karol Wojtyla undoubtedly knew of it. He was ordained in November 1946 and at once went for two years to Rome to obtain a doctorate in theology from the Dominican university there. He wrote a thesis on John of the Cross's understanding of the act of faith and

---

[44] See below, p. 137.
[45] In this section I have drawn on Hellman, "John Paul II and the Personalist Movement" and on Dulles, *The Splendor of Faith*.

it he emphasised "the personal nature of the human encounter with God".[46] He lived with the seminarians in the Belgian college, who knew about what was going on in France and Belgium, and he spent the summer vacation of 1947 in those countries. In June 1948 he obtained his doctorate and returned to Poland, where for three years he did pastoral work and then he had two years study leave to obtain a higher doctorate which would qualify him for academic work in Poland. He wanted to work on what is the fundamental basis of morality, he did not believe that he would find the answer to this question in Neo-Scholasticism, and at the suggestion of a former mentor he decided to work on Scheler, which he did with great difficulty.[47] His thesis was *An Evaluation of the Possibility of Constructing a Christian Ethics on the Basis of the System of Max Scheler.* His judgement was that it was not possible to do this but, as we shall see, he did not reject Personalism.

It has been said that the school of philosophy in the Catholic University of Lublin, under the leadership of Mieczslaw Krapiec OP, set out to develop a new philosophy from the Thomism of Maritain and Gilson, the Existentialism of Heidegger, Jaspers and Buber, and the phenomenology of Scheler and Roman Ingarden. To these should be added the Personalism of Mounier. The participants in this project maintained that thinking should begin with the human person, for which reason their philosophy is called, among other things, Lublin Existential Personalism. In October 1953 Wojtyla became a lecturer in this school and he participated in the further development of its doctrine.

In September 1958 he was made a bishop and in 1958-59 he gave lectures in which, as he said, he endeavoured to replace the old argument against contraception—that it is an interference with nature and therefore immoral—with a new one, that it involves the immoral use of one person by another.[48] When it was announced that there would be a council and committees were appointed to write draft decrees for it, he sent a nine-page document in which he said that Christian

---

[46] Weigel, *Witness to Hope,* p. 85.
[47] See above, pp. 57-59.
[48] These lectures were published as a book in 1960, and in 1981 they appeared in English as *Love and Responsibility.*

Personalism should be the foundation of all ethics.[49] Which brings me to Vatican II.

Vatican II

Begnning in 1962, Vatican II was held. I shall leave its properly theological decisions aside and simply say that, intellectually dominated by members of the movements which I mentioned above, it produced one Personalist constitution or decree after another. In its decree on ecumenism it said that the co-operation of all Christians "should contribute to a just appreciation of the dignity of the human person".[50] In the decree on bishops it said that bishops should teach how seriously the Church regards earthly [i.e., secular] realities, and the first mentioned is "the human person in his freedom and bodily life".[51] The mention of bodily life shows that the word "person" was understood as Mounier understood it, as meaning the whole human being and not only his or her soul. The decree on education argued that all human beings have the dignity of persons and hence a right to education.[52] If earlier Catholic writers had wished to demonstrate that education should at least be offered to all human beings, they would have said either that it is demanded by human nature as rational or that the common good requires that all citizens be educated, but by the early sixties the dignity of the person had become the first principle of ethics in the Church. By the end of the council, Personalism was completely in possession. The decree on religious liberty begins with the words "Dignitatis personae humanae", which were intended to express its essence, and its argument proceeds from the respect due to persons. Finally and most especially, the decree on *The Church in the World of This Time* states its fundamental ethical princple in a chapter entitled "The Dignity of the Human Person" and it proceeds to apply that principle in its discussion of the principal aspects of contemporary life.[53]

---

[49] See Dulles, *The Splendor of Faith*, p. 5.
[50] Vatican II, *Unitatis Redintegratio*, # 12.
[51] Vatican II, *Christus Dominus*, # 12.
[52] Vatican II, *Gravissimum Educationis*, # 1.
[53] In an article published in 1997-98, Koblier says: "Vatican II witnesses to a great paradigm-shift from Neo-Scholastic conceptualism to the existentialism typical of German theology after the nineteen-thirties" ("Vatican

After Vatican II to 1978

After the council, Personalism held the ground it had won and Paul VI's encyclicals on ethical issues were Personalistic and in this respect markedly different from pre-war encyclicals on the same subjects. For instance, whereas *Quadragesimo Anno* (1931) of Pius XI said virtually nothing about persons, Paul VI's *Populorum Progressio* (1967) said: "Any human society ... must lay down as a foundation this principle, namely that every human being is a person", and it constantly refers to the dignity of persons; and whereas *Casti Connubii* (1930), on sexual morality, hardly mentions persons, *Humanae Vitae* (1968) talks about "the person of woman", "married persons" and "mutual personal perfection". What was hardly mentioned in the earlier encyclicals is in the later ones the basis of the teaching.

Karol Wojtyla was a Personalist when he went to Vatican II and he has said that "his participation in the proceedings stimulated and inspired his thinking about the person". He subsequently wrote *The Acting Person*, which is an attempt to work out the basic theory of Lublin Personalism in a systematic way.

From 1978

In 1978 Karol Wojtyla became pope and he has been a Personalist pope.[54] William B. Smith says:

II as a Program in Applied Philosophy", p. 320). Like the authors whom I mentioned earlier, he has confused personalism with existentialism.

[54] Dulles says this in *The Splendor of Faith: The Theological Vision of Pope John Paul II*. See especially the sections headed "Personalism" (pp. 21-22) and "Personalist Principles" (pp. 133-134). In *Witness to Hope*, his life of John Paul II, Weigel says that "the Lublin project" was concerned with "the true liberation of the human person" and that it was agreed that "thinking should commence with the human person" (p. 133), and he says that when he wrote his second thesis "it was Scheler's personalism ... that Wojtyla found most attractive" (p. 128), but Weigel does not use the term "personalism" of either Lublin or Wojtyla and neither personalism nor Mounier is in the index to the book. He prefers to use the word "humanism": for instance, of the essay which Wojtyla sent to the Vatican II preparatory commission, saying that personalism should be the basis of Christian ethics, Weigel says that it was "an essay on the crisis of humanism" (p. 145).

Chapter 3: *A History of Personalism*

The personalism of John Paul is the only possible point of departure for understanding his thought on man and woman. His personalism underlies and informs all his teaching on "fair love", as it underlies and informs all the other regions of his teaching. When John Paul speaks of the "anthropological basis" of his teachings, he is referring to this underlying personalism. Much that seems puzzling in John Paul's teaching becomes intelligible as soon as it is traced back to its personalist foundations.[55]

In *Familiaris Consortio* (1981) he repeated the Personalist argument against contraception which he had used in his lectures of 1958-59 and in his encyclical on work (1981) he talked about work and the person. Finally, just as Mounier in 1930 hoped that out of the economic crisis of that time a new economic system would arise that would be neither capitalist nor Communist but Personalist; so when Communism ended in Eastern Europe John Paul II hoped that a new order would emerge which would be neither capitalist nor Communist.

Some important thinkers and Personalism

In conclusion, I want to deal briefly with a few thinkers who were in different ways related to Personalism. The first, Martin Buber, was a Jew, two were Catholic laymen and three were Jesuits.

Martin Buber (1878-1965)

Martin Buber wrote *I and Thou* in Vienna between 1916 and 1922 and it was published there in 1923 (an English translation appeared in 1937). Buber said personalist things in another language. Where a personalist might say that we become fully persons only through communication with other persons, Buber says: "Through the Thou a man becomes I",[56] a formula which is short and sticks in the mind but is not immediately intelligible to anyone who has not got the hang of Buber's way of talking. Buber does use the word "person" in two places in this book. On pp. 44-51 he uses "personal" as the opposite of "public"[57] and on pp. 62-65 he makes a distinction between individuality (*Eigenwesen*) and person (*Person* in German). He says:

---

[55] Smith, "John Paul's Vision of Sexuality and Marriage", p. 54.
[56] Buber, *I and Thou*, p. 62.
[57] See above, p. 48.

The I of the primary word I-Thou makes its appearance as person and becomes conscious of itself as subject.... Individuality makes its appearance by being differentiated from other individualities. A person makes his appearance by entering into relation with other persons.[58]

He also says: "The person becomes conscious of himself as sharing in being, as co-existing, and thus as being,"[59] and: "The stronger the I of the primary word I-Thou is in the twofold I, the more personal is the man".[60] Here, for a short time, Buber expresses in personalist language ideas which, in any language, are personalist. I think that if Buber had known of the Personalists of that time he would have been able to express many of his thoughts more simply, and perhaps we would have been the poorer for it.

Jacques Maritain (1882-1973)

After 1934, Maritain continued to insist on the distinction between individuality and personality which he had made in *Three Reformers* (1925). He gave some lectures in Spain which in 1936 he published, with revisions, as *Integral Humanism*; it was close in spirit to Mounier's *Personalist Manifesto,* published in the same year, but it was not a Personalist book. In 1939 he gave a lecture in Oxford on "The Human Person and Society", in 1945 he gave a lecture in Rome on "The Person and the Individual" and in 1946 he put these together, added to them, and published *The Person and the Common Good,* in which he proposed a "Thomistic personalism".[61] By this time had written many Thomist books in French, they had been translated into many languages, and he had become perhaps the best-known Thomist in the world.

A human being, Maritain said, can be regarded either as an individual or as a person. According to Thomas, he said, matter is the principle of individuality,[62] so that as an individual a human being tends to be materialistic, self-centred and grasping. Spirit, however, is

---

[58] Buber, *I and Thou*, p. 62.
[59] Ibid., p. 63.
[60] Ibid., p. 65.
[61] Maritain, *The Person and the Common Good*, p. 13.
[62] See below, p. 92.

Chapter 3: *A History of Personalism*

the principle of personality so that as a person a human being is "related to an infinitely greater good—the divine transcendent Whole".[63] Maritain drew ethical conclusions from this. He said that "evil arises when, in our action, we give preponderance to the individual aspect of our being".[64] To develop oneself as an *individual*, he said, "is to live the egoistical life of the passions, to make oneself the centre of everything".[65] Instead, we should live as *persons*, being spiritual and seeking God above all things.

Maritain also said that as an individual a particular human being is inferior in value to the society to which he or she belongs, and he said that a human being in a society is "as an individual or part, inferior to the whole and must, as an organ of the whole, serve the common work";[66] a human being "as an individual is necessarily bound, by constraint if need be, to serve the community and the common good since it is excelled by them as the part by the whole";[67] "the individual in each one of us, taken as an individual member of the city, exists for his city, and ought at need to sacrifice his life for it, as for instance in a just war".[68] However, he said, the civil society should bear in mind that human beings are also persons, involved in a higher reality, and the state should respect any demands that the higher reality may make of them: in this sense, the Christian city is "fundamentally personalist". For Maritain, one may perhaps say, the leaders of civil society are analogous to the coaches of sports teams in a boys school, who as coaches work on the principle that it is the teams, not individual boys, that matter (ideally, when they select boys or move them around it is for the sake of the teams, not for the benefit of particular boys), and they train them always to think of the good of the team, not of their own personal glory; however, ideally they know that what goes on in the classrooms and library is of greater importance than sport, that at times the demands of study must take precedence over the wishes

---

[63] Maritain, *The Person and the Common Good*, p. 18.
[64] Ibid., p. 43.
[65] Maritain, *Three Reformers*, p. 24, quoting Garrigou-Lagrange.
[66] Maritain, *The Person and the Common Good*, p. 70.
[67] Ibid., p. 77.
[68] Maritain, *Three Reformers*, p. 22. "City" means not Paris or London but any big secular society, for example a nation.

of the sportsmasters, and that at the higher level every boy matters for his own sake.

According to Mounier and Personalists generally, and to many others, Maritain made a mistake when he built a whole theory, including a theory of the state, on the distinction between individual and person, since (as Boethius in the sixth century saw) individuality is an element of personhood. Also, when Personalists say that workers, sick people and old people should be treated as persons, they do not mean only that it should be borne in mind that they have a religious destiny which transcends this world, they mean that *as beings of this world* they must be treated with respect. Finally, Maritain was a Thomist, Mounier was not, and as Mounier developed, the difference between them became apparent. That Maritain did not accept Mounier's Personalism may explain the opposition to the post-Vatican-II church which he manifested in *The Peasant of the Garonne*.

Pierre Teilhard de Chardin (1881-1955)

In 1950 Teilhard de Chardin said that when he was a boy "powerful was the fascination that the Impersonal and the Generalised had for me".[69] This undoubtedly led him to become a scientist and in his early writings he often gives the impression that he did not care about individuals or, as we would now say, about persons. In the nineteen-twenties he saw that human history is a continuation of zoological evolution and he said that each of us must make a choice: either to seek his or her own individual fulfilment, or else to put that out of mind and work for the universe as a whole; and he said that the latter is the right course to choose. He was on a line of thinking that leads towards a depreciation of individual persons like you and me.

He had, however, been brought up, and as a Jesuit he lived, in a religious and social milieu which emphasised individuals, and he said in 1915 that Christian teaching insists on "the primacy over everything of souls, that is, of individual centres".[70] At around the same time he said:

> There is a tendency to make progressively more allowance for the freedom of the individual, and this because there is a general

[69] Teilhard, "The Heart of Matter", in *The Heart of Matter*, p. 58.
[70] Teilhard, *The Making of a Mind*, p. 64.

awareness of the respect to which the unique and incommunicable development of every soul is entitled.[71]

(One notices that he talks of "souls" here where we would now say "persons".[72]) There was thus a certain conflict in him between his science and his religion, with the religion working like a brake on his meta-scientific speculations.

In the winter of 1928-29 he went through a crisis and soon afterwards he said that the idea of the person was "rapidly taking on an extraordinarily increasing importance in my view of the world".[73] He saw at last that the individual and the communal or universal are in personal life not opposed but linked, and he began to picture evolution as a bringing of persons into close unions in which they are not destroyed but, on the contrary, strongly affirmed as distinct individuals. Thus his conflict disappeared, the brake was taken off and a new period of creative writing began for him as he developed this and associated ideas in a series of articles written during the nineteen-thirties.[74] Among them is one entitled "Sketch of a Personalistic Universe" (1936), in which he says that there is no better, indeed no other, natural centre of the total coherence of things besides the human person. Working backwards from the human person, he said, one sees the cosmos dissolving; working forwards towards the person one sees it being made. And, he said, when things are seen in terms of the person, false oppositions between spirit and matter, and universality and personality, vanish.[75]

[71] Teilhard, "Mastery of the World and the Kingdom of God", in *Writings in Time of War*, p. 77.
[72] See above, p. 49.
[73] Teilhard, letter of 15 July 1929, quoted in Cuénot, *Teilhard de Chardin*, p. 260n. In a letter to Léontine Zanta written a few weeks later he talked of "the extraordinary development that the notion or value of the 'person' has taken in my intellectual construction" (letter of 23 August 1929). These letters were written from China but Teilhard was in Paris from October 1927 to November 1928 and he may have picked up the idea then and later seen the significance of it.
[74] These essays have been brought together and published as *Human Energy* and *Activation of Energy*.
[75] Teilhard, "Sketch of a Personalistic Universe", *Human Energy*, p. 90. Teilhard entitled this article "Esquisse d'un univers personnel", to which he added, in English, "A Personalistic Universe".

During the nineteen-thirties, when Mounier's Personalist movement was growing and being talked about in France, Teilhard was in China and to a large extent out of touch with what was going on at home. He was even more out of touch during the years of World War II, when he was in Japanese-occupied Peking (as the city was then called). In May 1946 he returned to Paris, where his main aim, and what was expected of him, was the presentation of his own ideas to the intellectual public. This he did for five years, during which he and Mounier, who had been prominent since the liberation, may have met and felt that there was some affinity between them,[76] but they worked separately, and when Mounier and Teilhard were both dead Mounier's successor Jean-Louis Domenach published in *Esprit* a critical article about Teilhard's personalism.[77]

Gabriel Marcel (1889-1973)

I must confess that while during the last fifty years I have read many of Marcel's writings I am not able to talk about him with confidence. He sometimes used the word "person" but in an offhand way, so that a book which lists the words he used, with explanations of them, does not include it. In 1940, probably because Mounier had been writing so much about person and action, Marcel published "Remarques sur les notions d'acte et de personne", in which he opposed person not to individual but to the French *on,* who is a faceless member of the mass of humanity. John B. O'Malley says that when he set out to study Marcel he found the concept of person forcing itself on him as the integrating focus of Marcel's philosophical investigations, and his book is *The Fellowship of Being: An Essay on the Concept of Person in the Philosophy of Gabriel Marcel.* I am willing to believe this, but Marcel did not himself use the word in that way and consequently I have not included him in the story of Personalism. Because of his use of the word "being", he was often said to be a Christian Existentialist, but that is not the same thing.

---

[76] Ligneul, *Teilhard and Personalism* is about the affinity between Mounier and Teilhard.
[77] Domenach, "Le personnalisme de Teilhard de Chardin".

Benard Lonergan (1900-1984)

In the chapter on the history of Scholasticism I mentioned Bernard Lonergan. In *Insight* (1957) he used the term "persona" for the image of himself which a man presents in public, opposing "the outer rind of the persona" to "the ego or *moi intime*"[78] and "the persona that appears before others" to "the more intimate ego".[79] "Persona" in this sense is not what a Personalist means by "person"; rather, what Lonergan calls the ego or *moi* (in English, the I) is the person, but in *Insight* Lonergan for some reason avoided that word. He also said that "everyone has his own personal reference frame" as opposed to the public reference frame;[80] this is not personalist talk, either. In a footnote on p. 731, which looks as if it was added after the book was written, he offered an excuse for omitting any discussion of personal relationships and this amounts to an admission of the fact that *Insight* shows no awareness whatever of the Personalist movement or of how the word "person" was being used by Personalists and others. Between *Insight* (1957) and *Method in Theology* (1972) he seems to have discovered Personalism since in *Method* he said that we go beyond acting "as intelligent" to a further dimension of being human, where "we emerge as persons"; he said that "there emerges in consciousness the significance of personal value and the meaning of personal responsibility", and that we exercise liberty in making "personal relations".[81] Thus "the person" was a major part of the advance which Lonergan made in the fifteen years between *Insight* and *Method in Theology*.

Karl Rahner (1904-1984)

In *Personal Becoming: Karl Rahner's Christian Anthropology*, Andrew Tallon has written an account of Karl Rahner's movement towards Personalism. In *Spirit in the World* (1939) Rahner talked about the human being not as a person but as a spirit or mind, and the world of the title was the material universe with no specific mention of persons. Also, the book dealt with the mind in a very general way. It was, then, impersonal. In 1941 Rahner wrote *Hearers of the Word* and

---

[78] Lonergan, *Insight*, p. 470. See above, p. 49.
[79] Ibid., p. 191.
[80] Ibid., p. 144.
[81] Lonergan, *Method in Theology*, pp. 10, 38, 48.

an article on concupiscence, in both of which he used the distinction between person and nature, and while he said, for instance, that "love is the self-luminous act of movement towards a person in his underived uniqueness",[82] and that human historicity is that of "a free being who subsists in himself, who within a society of persons like himself experiences the total realisation of this personal essence in space and time",[83] he did not pursue this line of thought. In 1957, in *On the Theology of Death,* he talked of the person but while he dealt with death as the separation of soul and body and as the end of "man's state of pilgrimage", it does not seem to have occurred to him that dying also means leaving other persons, whom one loves. Tallon says that he had an "impersonal personalism", that is, he used the term "person" but rarely in a Personalist way.[84] It is perhaps strange that so long after Buber (who wrote *I and Thou* in Vienna around 1920), Ferdinand Ebner (whose similar book was published in Innsbruck in 1921) and Scheler (who was famous), Rahner was unaware of Personalism. However, Tallon says that in the nineteen-sixties, just before and during Vatican II, in articles about love and guilt, Rahner advanced towards "a truly (overdue) interpersonal concept of person and becoming.[85]

---

[82] Rahner, *Hearers of the Word,* # 8, p. 100 (second German edition, p. 123).

[83] Ibid., # 11, p. 134 (German, p. 165). The translator of this book introduces the word "person" in some places where it does not appear in the original (for instance, "Wer als Freier vor einem Anderen steht" is translated as "Whoever stands as one free person before another" (ibid., # 7, German p. 116), with the result that the book seems more personalist in English than in German.

[84] Tallon, *Personal Becoming,* p. 165.

[85] Ibid., p. 118. The articles on love and guilt are a 1961 article on love in *Theological Investigations,* vol. 5, a 1963 article on guilt in vol. 6 and a 1965 article on love in vol. 6.

Part II

Scholastic philosophy and personalism

I have given outlines of the histories of Scholasticism and Personalism without presenting their ideas in a systematic way. I shall now summarise the philosophical ideas of these two thought-systems, mainly with the aim of pointing out differences between them. I shall deal here with moral-theological questions, since for the most part Catholic moral-theological positions are derived from ethical considerations.

Chapter 4

Neo-Scholastic Philosophy and Personalism as a Philosophy in General

SCHOLASTICISM

Being

Scholastic philosophers defined philosophy as the study of being as being (in Latin, *ens in quantum ens*) and *being* was their most fundamental concept.[1] When a Scholastic philosopher was explaining something in terms of "the principles of being" (to which I shall come), he had the feeling that he was offering the ultimate explanation of it, and a principal first-year subject in courses of Scholastic philosophy was ontology, which was the study of being.

The four causes

Scholastics talked about "the four causes". By "causes" they meant not what we now mean when we use the word but the things which we need to know in order to understand something: what it is (its "formal cause"), what it is made of (its "material cause"), who or what produced it (its "efficient cause", or cause in our usual sense of the word), and what it is for (its purpose or "final cause").

---

[1] McCool says: "A philosophy of being lies at the heart of every medieval Christian philosophy and defines its distinctive character" (*From Unity to Pluralism*, p. 179). In *the Spirit of Mediaeval Philosophy* Gilson begins his exposition of medieval philosophy with two chapters on being and beings.

The Scholastics believed that absolutely everything has a purpose, and that we do not understand anything completely unless we know what it is for. They distinguished between what they called the *finis operis* or "the natural purpose of the work" and the *finis operantis* or "the purpose of the agent". These are not necessarily the same: if, for instance, the natural purpose of drinking is the sustenance of the body, when someone drinks a toast the purpose of the agent is different.

Act and potency in Scholasticism

In classical physics, particles were the ultimate reality and events were explained *ultimately* in terms of particles and the laws of physics. If you had asked a physicist why the laws of physics were what they are, he would have said that explanations must start from something which is just given and the primary laws of physics are simply "given".

From Aristotle the Scholastics took the concepts which have come into English as "potency and act". They maintained that these are the fundamental principles of being, as particles were in classical physics. The first of the Twenty-Four Theses is: "Potency and act so divide being that whatever is is either pure act or it must be a combination of potency and act as intrinsic principles".[2] At one end of the scale of being, they said, is God, who is pure act, with no potency at all in him: that is, God is not *potentially* anything, he is *actually* everything positive there is. At the bottom is pure potency, which is not actually anything and hence does not actually exist on its own. Between God and pure potency are all created beings, who or which are combinations of act and potency, and a Scholastic principle was that two entities unite only when they combine as act and potency. Rousselot, for instance, said:

> This is a principle of St Thomas's metaphysics: each time two beings unite so as to form an assemblage that is truly unified [*un*], the relations between the two constituents are those of the determinant

---

[2] "*Potentia et actus ita dividunt ens, ut quidquid est, vel sit actus purus, vel ex potentia et actu tamquam primis et intrinsecis principiis necessario coalescat.*" See above, p. 33.
[3] Rousselot, *The Problem of Love*, p. 113n. .

Chapter 4: *Neo-Scholastic Philosophy & Personalism as a Philosophy* 89

and the determined; one is as it were the matter [potency] and the other the form [act].³

The love of unity

The unity of being

The Scholastics were not monist, far from it. In particular, they were highly conscious of the fact that God and creatures are distinct from each other and extremely different. They were also conscious of the fact that there are different human beings and that we, animals, plants and inorganic things are different. However, they had a love of unity.

One of the first theses in Neo-Scholastic textbooks was: "Being is one, true and good". That being is one meant that there is order within each being, by virtue of which its parts make one whole. It also meant that there is order between beings, so that they are not like a pile of unsorted books but, rather, like the books in a library which make up a collection and which, because there is order in them, can be talked about in the singular as "the collection".

Physicists assume that the whole material universe is governed by the same laws and has the same physical constants, which means that they explore, and seek to find the laws of, not merely a portion of the universe but all of it. In a similar way, Scholastic philosophers assumed that absolutely all beings are either pure act or combinations of potency and act, and they are all "governed" by the same principles of being, which are "given" to all beings. God himself has no choice but to accept his own nature as pure act and it is impossible for him to do anything which would be incompatible with being pure act. In this way being—all being—is one.

Loving unity as they did, the Thomists consistently preferred the general to the particular and worked in general terms: for instance, if they were talking about free will they talked about the intellect doing this and the will doing something else, not about an individual man or woman making a particular important decision. Also, Thomists said that the object of the intellect is not "the singular" or particular beings as such but their universal natures or essences, and they said that the proper object of the human intellect in this life is "the essences of material beings". Lonergan is extremely clear and emphatic about this. In *Verbum* he says that the proper object of the intellect is the quiddity or whatness of things, and "this quiddity prescinds from individual matter, for individual matter is not intelligible in itself but only in its relation to the *per se* universality of forms which it individuates".[4] In *Insight* he says that when we know something we intellectually abstract its general nature from it, leaving what he calls the empirical residue; and, he says, "individuality pertains to the empirical residue".[5] He also says:

> From the very structure of our cognitional apparatus, particulars are known through our senses, and our senses operate under spatio-temporal conditions. They cannot escape relativity and so, if an absolute is wanted, it must be sought on the level of intelligence which by abstraction from particulars provides a ground for invariant expressions.[6]

That is, while at the sensory level we deal with particular beings, at the spiritual level we are concerned only with general natures.

Unity in causation

According to the Scholastics, all beings are causally linked. Regarding the efficient cause, a series of Scholastic principles states: "No one gives what he does not have", "Nothing is in an effect which was not previously in its cause", 'That because of which something is as it is is like that itself, only more so", and "A cause is superior to its effect". This implied that when an efficient cause produces an effect, which then or later produces another effect, and so on, the way is always downhill.[7] In harmony with this the scholastics maintained that in

---

[4] Lonergan, *Verbum*, p. 193.
[5] Lonergan, *Insight*, p. 37.
[6] Ibid., p. 158.
[7] Here are the principles in Latin: *Nemo dat quod non habet, Nil in effectu quod non prius in causa, Propter quod unumquodque tale et illud magis, Causa superat effectum.* These principles were used in the debate over evolution: it was said that life cannot come from non-living beings, and rational animals cannot come from non-rational animals, because nothing can be in the product that was not in the source. The principles would seem to imply that students are always inferior to their teachers, so that the educational level of the human race keeps going down, but the Scholastics said that in these principles the term "cause" means the comprehensive cause, which includes God, who is infinite in all perfections, so that students can be better than their teachers and progress is possible.

any category the greatest is the efficient cause of the inferiors. The sun, for instance, is the hottest body in the universe and all other hot bodies get their heat ultimately from it. If in a religious community you find that a remarkably high number of people can speak Italian well, find the person who speaks Italian best and you will have found the source of this ability in others. That, anyway, was the idea. Also, they believed that every series of causes and effects stems from the same first cause, who or which is God.

Moreover, they maintained that in the order of final causality the greatest is the ultimate final cause of the inferiors: that is, ultimately, inferior beings exist for beings above them. One may see this in many machines: the sparkplug's purpose is to ignite the vapour in the cylinder, the purpose of which is to cause the axle to turn, and so on, in an ascending order. One sees it also in many organisations: the cleaners maintain the offices in which secretaries work, the secretaries serve the executives above them, lower executives work for higher executives and so on until one reaches the person at the top. The Scholastics saw this order in the natural universe and judged that plants exist to be eaten by animals, which exist to be eaten and in other ways used by human beings; also, lesser human beings have as their purpose the service of those who are greater. They had a strong sense of rank and order and they believed that just as there is ultimately one first efficient cause, so there is ultimately one ultimately final cause, God.

The other transcendentals

One, true and good were said by the scholastics to be the three transcendental or universal properties of being. That every being is true meant that every being is intelligible. That is, whereas there are many beings which simply cannot be seen, even with a telescope or microscope, because the eye is limited in what it can see, there is no being which cannot be known intellectually. Usually, the search for understanding began with a search for unity of some kind: for instance, to take an obvious case, if one wanted to understand something one put it with many others in a class of beings, and one then explained it as a member of that class.

Later, when I discuss value, I shall say what was meant by "every being is good".

Material beings

Substantial form and prime matter

According to the Scholastics, material beings are essentially composed of substantial form and prime matter, which combine as act and potency. In all material beings other than human beings, it is the composite which comes into existence and which then exists; the form has no existence of its own but exists only as an element of a material being. When a non-human material being ceases to exist, the form simply vanishes and its place in the matter is taken by other substantial forms. For instance, when an ainimal dies, its substantial form vanishes and the matter is informed by millions of forms of a lower kind; the resulting millions of distinct beings interact with one another, with the result that the body decomposes.

The principle of individuation

The Thomists maintained that matter is what they called "the principle of individuation": that is, a material species is distinguished from others by the form, but within a species one individual is distinguished from others by matter. They concluded that since angels do not have matter, each angel is a whole species. Both Scotus and Suarez differered from the Thomists on this.

The human being

The definition

To define anything scholastics looked for a larger class of beings to which it belonged and then they looked for what most basically made it different from other beings of that class. They defined *human being* by putting us in the general class of animals[8] and then looking for what, most fundamentally, makes us different from other animals. We differ from other animals in that we laugh and wear clothes but they would not have defined the human being as the laughing animal

---

[8] We now do not generally use the word "animal" of human beings. The definition above is from a time when we were classed as animals.

or the clothed animal because neither laughter nor clothing is what *fundamentally* makes us different. They would also have rejected "animal with free will" and "loving animal" because free will and love presuppose intellect, which is therefore more fundamental, and they decided that the basic difference between human beings and other animals is intellect or reason and they defined the human being as the rational animal.

This showed that they believed quite strongly in the human body, with its animal functions and senses, as an essential element of the human being, not a thing which he or she possesses. In their worldview there was a vast difference between human beings and pure spirits such as angels. At the same time they affirmed an essential difference between human beings and other animals.

Human nature

There is this difference between human beings and other material beings, including non-rational animals: the human substantial form, or soul, is "specially created", it is spiritual, it owns its existence, and it continues to exist after it separates from matter.

The Scholastics commonly maintained that human souls are created as individual entities (I do not say "beings" since there is only one being, the complete human being who is a composite of soul and body). That is, human souls and hence human beings are not individuated by prime matter, as all other material beings are. (This might seem to have implied that each human soul is a whole species, but they did not say that.)

The intellect and the will

A human being enjoys a spiritual consciousness, which has two faculties, and his or her main purpose in life is to possess being. The most basic spiritual faculty is the intellect and our primary purpose is to possess being by knowing it. The other faculty is the will, and we possess being, secondarily, by willing it. It was maintained that the formal object of the will is "being as good" so that when we see intellectually that a being is good, we can will it.

Neo-Scholastics and "the person"

If the word "person" had not been used in theology, in connection with the Trinity and the Incarnation, it might never have been used in Scholastic Philosophy, but since most students of this philosophy were going to study theology later the professors felt a need to define it philosophically and to explain the definition, so that the students would know what the word meant when, later, they met it in theology. Wojtyla says that in Thomas's system "person complies with theological function",[9] which being translated means that, having defined the term, the Neo-Scholastics did not talk about the person in philosophy.

They started with Boethius's ancient definition of a person as "an individual substance of a rational nature" (*naturae rationalis individua substantia*).[10] Thomas Aquinas modified this, saying that a person is a subsistent with a rational nature[11] or an individual with a rational nature.[12] He emphasised individuality, saying that qualities are individuated by the substances in which they inhere (the whiteness of a white thing is a particular whiteness because it is that of a particular thing) whereas substances are individual in their own right, and he went on to say that because rational substances are *more* individual than non-rational substances there is a special word, person, for them.[13] In Neo-Scholastic times, Louis de Raeymaeker said that what formally constitutes a person is its own substantial existence.[14] Billot said that subsistence is what makes an intellectual being a person and "by subsistence is meant what in reality and actually has its own existence in itself".[15] There are two things here: first, individuality, as in "incommunicable", "individual" and "its own"; second, subsistence, which is

---

[9] Wojtyla, "Thomistic Personalism", quoted from the Polish in *Existential Personalism,* p. 44.
[10] Boethius, *De duabus naturis,* chap 3, *PL,* 64,1343. Boethius (480-525) was a Roman who studied in Athens but lived and wrote in Rome.
[11] "*Subsistens in natura rationali*" (Thomas, *Summa Theologica,* 1 29 3 c).
[12] "*Individuum rationalis naturae*" (ibid., ad 2).
[13] "*Speciale nomen habent singularia rationalis naturae. Et hoc nomen est persona.*" (Ibid., 1 29 1 c.)
[14] "*Esse proprium substantiale*" (de Raeymaeker, *Metaphysica Generalis,* pp. 177-178).
[15] "*Nomen subsistentiae [significatur] id quod re etiam et actu habet esse in se*" (Billot, *De Verbo Incarnato,* p. 63).

not the same as existence because it is the existence *of an individual.* Rational or intellectual nature is a condition.

They said that a person is a whole being, not a part of a being. Not using in this context the word "person", Thomas said: "My soul is not *I*" so that if only "my soul attains salvation in another life, I will not attain it".[16]

Personalism

What "the person" means in Personalism

As my short history of Personalism made clear, it is an ensemble of ideas about how we should live rather than a theory which explains the universe. Personalists do not go in for defining their terms but it is possible, I believe, to say what they mean by "person". As a personalist definition of "person" I propose: *Who says I and to whom Thou is said.*[17] Since Personalism is an agent philosophy, it considers not so much what a person is as what it means to be, and to treat someone as, a person.

Almost every existing being is both a unique particular being and one of a kind, and he, she or it can be looked at in either way. If, for instance, a friend asks me to lend him a hundred dollars and I hand him a hundred-dollar note, when he pays back the loan I do not say, "But this is not the note I lent to you, it is a different one". This is because while I handed him a particular note I did not regard it as particular but as one of a kind of notes. Suppose, however, that after working for a year in a parish I had to leave and, on leaving, I was given a pair of silver cuff links. If later someone needed a pair of cuff links and I lent him these, I would be distressed if he lost them and gave me a similar pair which he had bought to replace them. This would obviously be because the cuff links had been precious to me not precisely as *cuff links* but as *particular things*, which as such were

---

[16] *"Anima mea non est ego. Unde licet anima consequatur salutem in alia vita, non tamen ego"* (Thomas, *Commentary on 1 Cor 15*, lect. 2).

[17] In the twelfth century Richard of St Victor, to whom I shall return when we come to the Trinity, said that if we ask "Who?", the answer is a particular person, whereas if we ask "What?", the answer is a nature, expressed in a general term. (See *De Trinitate*, IV,7, *PL*,196,935A).

irreplaceable. A human person is a human being who is regarded as a *particular* human being. Suppose that someone appreciates a woman secretary because she is willing, efficient and always cheerful. If this woman says to herself, "If I leave and my place is taken by another who is equally willing, efficient and cheerful, my employer will hardly notice the change", what this means is that she believes that she is not appreciated *as a person*. She may say: "He (or she) appreciates my qualities but not *me*". On the other hand, a man who is in love with a beautiful woman may appreciate her not so much as *a beautiful woman* but as *this person,* who happens to be beautiful, and whose beauty he appreciates mainly because it is hers. In this respect the Personalist idea of person is not entirely different from the Scholastic idea, of which, as we saw, individuality is of the essence.

Also, a person is an *actually existing* rational being. If, then, a couple discuss whether or not to have another child, they are not talking about a person, which is why they talk about having *a child,* not about having *Jim* or *Kate* (and this is not only because they do know whether, if they have a child, it will be a boy or a girl). Later, if they have a child, who exists, he or she is a person. In insisting on what they called "subsistence", the Scholastics were saying this.

Moreover, many thinkers have identified themselves as persons with their souls and regarded their bodies as being like vehicles in which they were enclosed and in which they moved around. John Donne, for instance, said:

> *Our bodies why we do we forbear?*
> *They are ours, though they are not we. We are*
> *The intelligences [minds within], they the spheres.*[18]

In 1969 H. D. Lewis wrote that a person *is* his or her mind ("my real self is my mind") and merely *has* a body.[19] A number of Boston Personalists wrote in this way but for most Personalists now the human person is a human being in his or her entirety, which means that to deal with people personally one must deal with both their spiritual and their bodily lives.

Finally, as I shall say in the next chapter, a person is usually a human being as a *subject*.

[18] Donne, "The Ecstasy".

Chapter 4: *Neo-Scholastic Philosophy & Personalism as a Philosophy* 97

LIKENESSES

Neo-Scholasticism and Personalism were both rational, though some philosophers dismissed Personalism as the outpouring of emotion. Also, whereas Boston Personalism was subjectivistic, Mounier's Personalism, which which I am mainly concerned here, is realistic, as was Neo-Scholasticism. Neither Neo-Scholastics nor Personalists were materialists and none of them believed that "person" stands for the human spirit as distinct from the body. Finally, in Catholic circles both of these philosophies were orthodox.

DIFFERENCES

Some differences

Neo-Scholasticism began in the Catholic Church and remained almost entirely within Catholic institutions. On the continent of Europe, Mounier's Personalism was mainly Catholic, while in the United States Boston Personalism was mainly Methodist.

Within the Catholic Church, Neo-Scholasticism was mainly an activity of priests and priests-to-be, who were required to study it in Latin. Not only did this make the institutions in which it was taught inaccessible to most brothers, nuns and laypeople, but it had technical terms which, even when they were translated, only scholastics could understand—terms like *species impressa* or "impressed species" were unintelligible to others. While some efforts were made to take Neo-Scholasticism to laypeople,[20] they had little success, except perhaps in the United States. Catholic Personalism, on the other hand, was originally a lay phenomenon; its periodicals were edited and largely written by laymen and laywomen, and they were for thinkers of all kinds.

The Neo-Scholastics introduced a subject, epistemology, to deal with what in the nineteenth century was a major philosophical problem, and in ethics they dealt with current issues, but they mainly looked back to the past. They especially looked to Thomas Aquinas, of whose

---

[19] H. D. Lewis, *The Elusive Mind*, p. 23.
[20] See above, p. 39.

works they produced scholarly editions, and they quoted him all the time. Also, though they were not always aware of this, they were greatly influenced by Second Scholasticism. The early Personalists, on the other hand, were for the most part conscious of being original and they were in the Present Age which was forming as they worked.

The Neo-Scholastics did not ignore the secular intellectual world but they tended to regard it as the domain of their "adversaries". They studied the writings of non-Scholastic philosophers, but usually in an adversarial spirit. They were not to the fore in accepting various modern scientific ideas, such as evolution and indeterminacy, or political ideas like democracy and religious freedom. Personalists, among whom I include the *Esprit* team and Dorothy Day, were more involved in the secular world and more positive in their attitude towards its movements.

Spectator and agent philosophies

Scholastic Philosophy was in the first place a spectator philosophy,[21] which appealed to people who enjoyed clear, impersonal analysis and who in many cases were ill at ease with personal talk. In 1929 the scientist J. D. Bernal said : "The same type of mind that would now make a physicist would in the Middle Ages have made a scholastic theologian",[22] to which one can add that the same type of mind made Scholastic philosophers at the time when he was writing. Intellectually gifted students for the priesthood who did not have this type of mind did not enjoy their studies, often gave much time to extracurricular cultural pursuits, did not become graduate students of philosophy or theology and rarely thought in Scholastic terms when they had to make decisions or counsel people. Personalism, on the other hand, was an agent philosophy, which appealed to a different type of mind.

The question of historical sense

There was a time when mathematical truths such as 2 + 2 = 4 and scientific laws such as that of Boyle had not been discovered, but once they were discovered they were passed on unchanged from each

---

[21] See above, p. 18.
[22] Bernal, *The World, the Flesh and the Devil*, p. 53.

Chapter 4: *Neo-Scholastic Philosophy & Personalism as a Philosophy* 99

generation to the next. Many Neo-Scholastics thought that all truths are like these. They thought that Aristotle discovered many of them, that there followed some centuries of confusion, then Christ revealed truths which were imperfectly understood. There followed centuries of searching and then Thomas Aquinas put almost everything in order, after which there was not much more to be done. *Aeterni Patris* said that human reason, "borne on the wings of Thomas can scarcely rise higher".[23] At least since the Middle Ages, the Neo-Scholastics thought, their philosophy had been the unchanging "perennial philosophy" of the Catholic Church. They quoted Thomas and other medieval and Second-Scholastic authors as if what they had written was written last week. In all this one can see an unawareness of the significance of history in human thought. Etienne Gilson said: "The indifference of St Thomas towards history was prodigious",[24] which means that this unawareness was a feature of Scholasticism from the beginning. Raymond Nogar, whom I have quoted before and who was a Thomist professor of philosophy in Rome, said: "Thomism, as a system, has one very basic shortcoming: it is a view of the universe and of man in which history is incidental".[25] Gerald McCool says that post-Reformation Scholastics "could not think historically" and that their method "could not handle history".[26] One scholastic philosopher actually referred to "that vulgar and contemptible thing which is actuality",[27] which put the subject-matter of history in its place.

Most scientists regard the history of science as history, not science, and when I studied science at Melbourne University the lecturers might introduce a topic with a few words about its history before going on to spend hours on what was known about it then.[28] In a similar way,

---

[23] Leo XIII, *Aeterni Patris* (1879), # 18.
[24] Gilson, "Cajetan et l'Humanisme théologique" in *Archives d'Histoire doctrinale et littéraire du Moyen-Age,* 1955, p. 133; quoted in Fessard, *De l'actualité historique*, I,20.
[25] Nogar, *The Lord of the Ab*surd, p. 93.
[26] McCool, *Nineteenth-Century Scholasticism*, p. 10.
[27] *"Cette chose vulgaire et méprisable qu'est l'actualité"* (P. J. de Tonquédec, *Les principes de la Philosophie Thomiste*, II,7; quoted in Fessard, *De l'actualité historique*, I,9).
[28] To be fair, I should say that the lecturers in modern physics often told us its history and led us through the historical development of knowledge about the atom, for instance.

while a course in Scholastic Philosophy usually included The History of Philosophy as a minor subject, the majors were devoted to what was believed to be timeless truth. Most Neo-Scholastics believed that for the most part non-Scholastic philosophic thought since the Middle Ages had been a long trip down a false route after a wrong turn taken by Descartes and that in a search for truth one should ignore it and return to Thomas.

As human persons are particular beings, each of whom has a history and is a member of the human race at a certain point in its history, Personalism is concerned not so much with unhistorical human nature as with particular persons in history. It is concerned with personal acts, which are always historical. Also, Personalist periodicals like *Esprit* and *Commonweal* deal with current issues, or the history which is being made now.

Chapter 5

Objective Reality and Subjectivity

Introduction

The meanings of the terms

By objective reality I mean what exists "in itself", independent of our thoughts and wishes. It sometimes means the whole ensemble of beings which exist in themselves, and it is thought of as a sort of *place* in which particular beings are situated, as "the past" is a sort of place in which past events are situated. When we first become conscious we find that objective reality is *there,* as it were thrown in front of us (which is what "ob-ject" means), and while we may be able to remove this or that particular thing we cannot remove reality as a whole. Nor can anyone else. Even God himself cannot bring it about that absolutely no one and nothing exists. A great deal of our intellectual growth and activity consists in increasing our knowledge of this whole ensemble. There are also, of course, *particular* objectively real beings. These include not only material beings but also spiritual beings. They also include physical laws: in a sense, Boyle's law exists in human minds but it states what always happens in the objective world. We shall see that they also include values.

By subjectivity I mean a person's consciousness or "mind and heart". Some of its elements are intellectual: these include knowledge, reasoning, puzzlement, judgements, certainty, doubt, ideas about possible things and events, and fantasies. They include many things which we know but are not thinking about all the time. Other elements are volitional: these include emotions, decisions, intentions, love, hate and repentance. Other elements, again, are "sensory". These include cognitive elements, such as the images of things we have seen, and non-cognitive elements such as physical pain and pleasure, fear and desire.

We now tend to use "the mind" for the intellectual part of subjectivity and "the heart" for the volitional part; when we want to talk about the whole of it, we talk, as I did in the previous paragraph, of "the mind and heart". In the gospels all subjectivity is called "the heart", so that when it is said that Mary kept the memory of the Finding in the Temple in her heart, this means that she had it constantly in her mind and had feelings about it, and when it is said that out of the heart come evil deeds, this means that wrongdoing originates in subjectivity. Sometimes now the word "soul" is used for all of subjectivity: a great-souled person is not someone with a great substantial form or a great mind and if someone says that there has been a meeting of souls this does not mean that two substantial forms have somehow made contact with each other or that there has been a meeting of minds only.

The room analogy: outside and inside

If a man is sitting in a room which has furniture in it, if in its walls there are windows and if outside the room there is a garden in which things are happening, the room with its contents is analogous to subjectivity and the garden outside in analogous to objective reality. This analogy is used when the terms "inner experience" and "outer reality" are used for subjectivity and objective reality. Also, objectively real things are sometimes said to be "outside the mind" or extramental.

The walls of the room do not represent one's skin. It is not the border between one's subjectivity and objective reality, since one's whole being is objectively real and in that sense "outside" one's mind.

Every normal adult human being, when awake, has a subjectivity. When a human being dies and the body is wheeled away, put into a refrigerator and eventually buried, this is not like what happens when a television set breaks down, is carried outside and eventually sent to the rubbish tip: in the human body, as not in the television set, a subjectivity has ceased to exist and we may say of a dead body that it is just a thing, with no one inside it.

The subconscious seems be neither objective nor in subjectivity, since what is in it is neither objectively real nor in subjectivity. In terms of the analogy above, it is like a basement underneath the room, which

Chapter 5: *Objective Reality & Subjectivity*

is not in the garden outside and which affects what goes on in the room without the person there being aware of it. Suffice it to say at this point that it is usually studied by psychologists.

The connections between objective reality and subjective experience

It is surely obvious that, while we can distinguish between an outside world and an inside world, they are not independent of one another. To a large extent the outside world is there first, and it affects what goes on in subjectivity: we observe objectively real beings, so that knowledge of them comes into subjectivity, and they often cause us to feel elated or dejected. On the other hand, we often think of things which do not exist, and we bring them into objectively real existence; also, we produce things, or we perform actions, the purpose of which is to express something which is subjective. In these cases, subjectivity precedes objectivity.

The study of subjectivity

In philosophical circles the word "phenomena" is now often used for the contents of subjectivity, and phenomenology is the study of subjective experiences. For instance, when Max Scheler wrote books about *ressentiment* and sympathy, he was working as a phenomenologist, so was Kierkegaard when he wrote about dread, and when Existentialists said that their method was phenomenological they meant that they were studying subjective experience.

Opposing preferences

Some people are more at home when looking at the objective world. In terms of the analogy, they spend nearly all their time looking out through the windows at what is going on in the garden. Others, while they see what is going on outside, prefer to give their attention to what is inside. One medical student, for instance, may come to the study of bone surgery, know at once that he has found his vocation and in due course become an orthopedic surgeon; another may find bones boring but be fascinated by what he learns about psychiatry, and he may in due course become a psychiatrist, who listens as people tell him about their thoughts and feelings. Some people enjoy films in which there is plenty of action and there are simple feelings like aggressivity and fear; other people do not find such films interesting, and go, instead, to films in which the important thing at any moment is what the characters are thinking and feeling, which is far from simple. The former films have a minimum of talk, the latter films have a lot of it. Also, at a dinner party some people are lively conversationalists so long as the talk is about practical "outside" matters like wine or the weather in different cities, but fall silent if someone begins to talk about anxiety or grief, while other people come alive at precisely such a time. Finally, in a school some bright children have good memories for facts, do well in science and find it hard to understand the point of poetry and novels, while the class in literature is the one that others most enjoy.

The tendency to think in one way or the other can reach extremes. I know a woman who was being treated by a psychiatrist for depression. She began to experience tiredness which the psychiatrist assumed was psychological in origin. As she had doubts about this, she went to a general practitioner, who carried out tests and found that her tiredness had a physical cause; she then cured her of it. On the other hand, if a man goes to see *Othello* and, when asked later what it was about, says: "There's a lot of talk and then a big black man strangles his wife", we may feel that the play was wasted on him. Ideally, one thinks in both ways, often at different times but sometimes in the same situation.

It may be true that awareness of objectivity and curiosity about it usually precedes awareness of subjectivity: one is first aware of the garden outside and then becomes aware of what is in the room. Growing children, for instance, having begun to talk, may refer to themselves in the third person and then, later, discover their inner selves (this has been called the *Icherlebnis* or discovery of the I) and for a time become excessively centred on these inner selves. Also, for many years science was concerned exclusively with what is objective and open to observation by anyone; it was not until the nineteenth century that subjective experience was studied in a systematic way and scientific psychology came into existence—and for many years it was not accepted by the scientific world at large. Moreover, it is said

Chapter 5: *Objective Reality & Subjectivity* 105

that, of people in a university who work in science or the arts, the scientists were usually younger than the arts-faculty people when they committed themselves to their life's work.

Cases where the distinction is made

When scholastic philosophers distinguished between the *finis operis* or the natural purpose of an action and the *finis operantis* or the purpose of the agent, they were distinguishing between the *objective* purpose of an action and the *subjective* aim of its agent.

Also, if we believe that moral obligations are objective, we nevertheless maintain that moral goodness is subjective. For instance, slavery is objectively immoral and it was and is a grave moral evil. However, when slavery had existed for generations in the American South, most white people believed that it was no more immoral to own human beings than to own horses, and many of them made sure that their horses and their slaves were well fed and not overworked. As moral goodness is subjective, these owners were morally good people and if actors have to play such persons (as an actor played Scarlett O'Hara's mother in *Gone With the Wind*), they ought not to play them as wicked people.

Neo-Scholasticism

The medieval philosophers were aware of subjectivity but they were more interested in objective reality and this is what they mainly meant by "being". The Neo-Scholastics were in this respect, as in others, true to their medieval heritage. They manifestly were like people who prefer to look out through the windows of their minds and they showed this in several ways. First, their course in ontology, which meant the study of being, was about objective reality, not subjective experience, and for them the word "ontological" meant "objectively real". Second, having observed sense perceptions and intellectual knowledge, they spent little time analysing them as subjective experiences but almost immediately asked what kind of being is capable of having such experiences and what goes on in the realm of objective reality when we have perceptions and make judgements. Thus they talked about the impressed species and the agent intellect, which according to them were objectively real and neither of which was in subjectivity. They said little about volitions as subjective experiences and did not analyse them in any detail; instead, they talked about the physical premotion or "concursus", which was pre-conscious. Third, as I have said, when they defined the word "person" they looked for something *objective* which would formally constitute it.[1] Fourth, they believed that in principle subjectivity ought to conform to objective reality. At the intellectual level, they said that the aim of the intellect is to obtain knowledge of being and that the truth, which is what we seek, is the conformity of the contents of the intellect, which are subjective, to being. As we shall see, at the volitional level, they believed that goodness consists in the conformity of the will to nature or being.

Personalism

With the Modern Age came a high awareness of subjectivity. In the sixteenth century Luther emphasised subjective and individual religious experience. So did Ignatius Loyola, for whom a spiritual exercise was a subjective experience, and the great mystics Teresa of Avila and John of the Cross, whose dark night of the soul was a subjective experience. In 1604-06 Shakespeare wrote *Othello, King Lear* and *Macbeth*, in which, while "outward" things happen, the main action takes place in men's subjectivities. As I said before, in 1637 Descartes launched modern philosophy with his "I think, therefore I am" or "I, a thinking subject, exist". Personalism is post-medieval and a fundamental difference between it and Neo-Scholasticism is that in it attention is primarily fixed on subjectivity. Every human being can be considered as an object, to be seen from outside (as it were, like a being outside in the garden), or as a subject, who has an inner life, and Personalists believe that to know someone as a person one must know him or her *as a subject*. If a man goes to a strip show, he looks at women as objects, not as subjects; he does not want to know anything about what they are thinking and feeling; which is to say that he does not see them *as persons*. If, on the other hand, a man in an office finds that a woman whom he has often seen is crying, asks her what the trouble is and she tells him about something that has happened to her and what as a subject she is feeling, he may suddenly and for the first time see her

---

[1] See above, p. 94.

Chapter 5: *Objective Reality & Subjectivity*

as a person. There is a difference here between the Scholastic and the Personalist idea: for the Scholastics, intellectuality is as it were the condition for being a person and it is not considered subjectively, whereas if I am right Personalists believe that to deal with someone as a person not only must he or she be an intellectual being but one must deal with him or her *as a subject.*

Personalists, then, are concerned with subjects. William B. Smith says of John Paul II:

> John Paul is constantly speaking of the "subjectivity" of persons. I doubt whether any previous pope ever spoke of subjectivity.... In one of his prepapal studies, Karol Wojtyla distinguishes between what he calls a predominantly "cosmological" understanding of man and a predominantly "personalist" understanding of him. In the former, man is considered from the outside.

To adopt a personalist approach, he says,

> one must stop looking at man from without and consider how he reveals himself to us from within, that is, how he lives his own being from his own inner centre. But this means that we adequately understand man as person only in understanding him in terms of his self-experience, or in other words his interiority.[2]

Unlike the Boston Personalists, many of whom identified the I with the inner subject and some of whom went further and professed subjectivism, Catholic personalists from Mounier on and from John Paul II down, while we stress persons as subjects, do so knowing that they are objectively real beings. Their actual existence is extremely important to us.

One problem with the Personalist emphasis on subjectivity, which I have not seen discussed, is that if it is taken very strictly only a human being who has a subjectivity is a person and has the rights of a person. This would seem to imply that a foetus, a child who has not reached the age at which it can in some sense think, and an adult who is in a coma are not persons. It could even be taken to mean that a sleeping human being is not a person. I would say that it is impossible to act in the manner of a properly personal relationship with any of these human beings, but the fact that there is an identity with a being who will be or has been a subject means that they can and should be treated as persons.

---

[2] Smith, "John Paul II's Vision of Sexuality and Marriage", pp. 64-65.

That person is higher than being

Neo-Scholastics usually believe that a cause is superior to its effect and, more generally, that if A is presupposed by B then A is superior to B. Now a human being as a subject presupposes him or her as an objectively real being, which on this principle implies that object is superior to subject. This, however, is not so and if one studies a human being as an objectively real being, with a human nature, and then goes on to study the subjective experiences of human beings, regarding them as persons, one moves up, not down. This means that a psychiatrist works with a human beings at a higher level than an orthopedic surgeon (in saying this I mean no offence to orthopedic surgeons, of the value of whose work I, who at diferent times have broken both wrists and both legs, and whose right wrist came out of plaster recently, am deeply appreciative) and Personalism is situated at a higher level of thought than Neo-Scholasticism. It also means that it is not always the role of subjectivity to adapt itself to objective reality, as it were obeying what is superior to it; on the contrary, subjectivity often has a life of its own and at other times, while not completely independent of objective factors, it at times controls objective reality and decides its nature.

Chapter 6

Free Will

What free will is

To say that a person in a particular situation has free will means two things. It means, first, that *more than one choice is possible*. For instance, when a billiard ball is heading towards a pocket it necessarily keeps on course and goes in, but if a man who has free will is walking towards a hotel it is possible for him to go into it and it is also possible for him to change his course and go past it. To say that a person has free will means, second, that *he or she makes the choice* and is therefore responsible for what happens. Thus the two elements of free will are multiple possibility and what is called self-determination and responsibility. As Wojtyla said, to understand free will we need to emphasise self-determination.[1]

While it was not often analysed or even stated, free will was generally assumed for centuries. In 1517, however, Luther denied it and in 1520 Pope Leo X condemned the denial of free will. Subsequently, Luther's followers did not follow him in denying free will but Calvin denied it and so did most of his followers. In the centuries which followed, many (not all) Protestants denied free will while all Catholics affirmed it. I will deal with this question here, because it is principally a philosophical one, but we must bear in mind that it was not a purely philosophical matter.

---

[1] Wojtyla said: "Any explanation of free will, if it is to conform to reality, must emphasise self-determination, and not consider only indifference [multiple possibility]... . Indifference has a secondary role, while self-determination has primary and fundamental significance." (*The Acting Person*, p. 121,)

Free will in Second Scholasticism

It was affirmed by all Second-Scholastic philosophers both that human beings have free will and that God has complete dominion over creatures so that his will is always done.[2] The philosophers had to find a way of reconciling these two statements. One attempt was made by Domingo Bañez (1524-1604), who said that prior to every act of the will a human being receives a "physical premotion" which moves him or her to perform a particular act. Sub-human beings, which do not have free will, when they are in a situation can do only one thing. The acts of human beings, however, he said in effect, are not determined by our natures or training or any natural laws, and this (he said) is what it means to say that we have free will. When, then, a human being is faced with a choice between two alternatives, God can give him or her a premotion to do either of them and he can do this without disturbing nature. The theory seems to me to be explicable in the following way. A dramatist writing a play, who wants all the events in it to be possible in our world, cannot have a character jump out of a high window and a few moments later walk into the room unharmed; but if in a play a husband tells his wife, whom he has hurt, that he is sorry for what he did, the dramatist can write either that she forgives him or that she refuses forgiveness, because both these actions are possible. Let us suppose that he or she writes that the wife forgives. When the play is performed, the wife of her own free will forgives her husband, and yet the whole thing has been decided by the author, who has control over what his characters do, though they have free will.

The Jesuits in Spain did not accept this theory and in 1582 a tremendous and disgracefully conducted battle began between them and the Dominicans, with members of the two orders denouncing each other in tirades from their pulpits. In 1588 a Jesuit in Portugal, Luis Molina, published a book with a different theory, according to which God, before he decides to create, knows exactly what every possible human being *would* do, of his or her own free will, in every situation he or she could possibly be in, and creates a universe knowing what

---

[2] See below, p. 155-156.

Chapter 6: *Free Will* 111

is going to happen in it. Thus God is in control and yet we freely decide.³ If I may put it this way, God is like a headmaster of a school who knows that if he were to ask Jones to decide the annual musical-theatre production it would be *The Mikado*, whereas if he were to ask Brown to make the decision it would be *Oklahoma!*; he chooses Brown, Brown makes a free decision (the headmaster does not order him to produce *Oklahoma!*) and puts on precisely the show that the headmaster decided would be put on. When this theory was published, the fighting became even more intense. The Vatican stepped in and eventually, in 1607, by which time Bañez and Molina were both dead, Pope Paul V made a decision in which he condemned neither of the opposing views as heretical and in effect opted for theological pluralism in the Catholic Church.

In the following centuries, the two orders went their separate ways, stopping just short of calling each other heretics. Each order stuck to its guns.

Neo-Scholasticism

In the early years of Neo-Scholasticism everyone knew of the disagreement between Jesuits and Dominicans but it was regarded as a case of agreeing on essentials while arguing about things which are not essential. After all, they all affirmed both human free will and divine dominion. Later, when there had been more study and argument, the difference between Banezianism and Molinism became clear and became an issue, especially when many Jesuits switched from Suarezianism to Thomism while remaining disciples of Molina, not Bañez. It became customary, in discussion of this question, for Dominicans to regard the theory of Bañez as an integral element of Thomism and to call it the Thomist theory, which would have meant that the Molinist Jesuits were not entitled to call themselves Thomists, and for Jesuits to call it not the Thomist but the Banezian theory.⁴

---

³ There has been a revival of interest in Molinism in philosophical circles.
⁴ See above, p. 41, where I said that when *The Twenty-Four Theses* of Thomism were issued in an effort to outlaw Suarezianism, the Banezian theory was not included.

Criticism of Neo-Scholasticism

At the risk of offending some Dominicans I will say that Bañez reconciled his theory of determinate physical premotion with belief in free will by equating free will with indeterminateness and not considering self-determination or, to use a word which dates from the seventeenth century and was not in the medieval or Second-Scholastic vocabulary, responsibility. In his theory, a man is not determined by his nature to do a particular thing, but it is God who actually decides which one is chosen, which means that the man does not determine the choice, God does, and God is ultimately responsible for what happens. In the analogy which I gave above, when the play is performed and the wife forgives her husband, this is because the author decided that this would happen; he is ultimately responsible. That is, Banezianism is incompatible with human free will, as this is now understood, so that a person could say: "When I decided to study philosophy rather than biology, both of these things were possible and in that sense I was free; I chose to study philosophy because God gave me a physical premotion to study it—he could have moved me to study biology, but he didn't. I, therefore, am not responsible for the choice which I made, he is."

Molinism was no better. In the example which I have given above, if a parent objects to the show which was put on and the headmaster replies, "I did not decide it, Brown did", the parent can reply: "You chose Brown as producer, knowing that he would produce *Oklahoma!*, so you in fact decided what would be performed, you are responsible for it", and there is no answer to this.

Any Neo-Scholastic who studied the problem found himself in a fog. A common final conclusion was: "It's a mystery".

Personalism

There is not a systematic Personalist metaphysics but some comments can be made from a more or less Personalist point of view. First of all, while all Scholastics and all Personalists affirm free will, the doctrine, if I may call it that, plays quite different roles in the two systems. For Scholastic metaphysicians, it is a kind of anomaly and in a sense a side-issue. For Personalists, it is a fundamental assumption.

Chapter 7

Value

Introduction

For a long time the word "value" was used mainly in its financial sense but late in the nineteenth century value-theory or axiology became a branch of philosophy. Courses were taught and books were written about it and before long almost everyone was talking about values, as they do now. For a long time Catholic philosophers did not talk about values, first, because the word "value" was not in their vocabulary and, second, because they associated it with a theory according to which all values are purely subjective. Instead, they talked, for instance, about the dignity rather than the value of the human person.

Moral obligations are derived from values and talk of values has now become a way of talking about morality, so that, for instance, people talk about family values rather than sexual ethics. An advantage of this change is that when one hear the word "morality" one tends to think of restrictions on one's freedom, but when one hears the word "value" one thinks in the first place of some reality which demands respect.

Bertrand Russell said in 1935 that "questions as to 'values' lie wholly outside the domain of knowledge"[1] and at around the same time the Logical Positivists in Vienna were saying that value judgements are meaningless because they cannot be empirically verified. It was hardly credible that the statement that something is good or bad is comparable to "hey diddle diddle", and a more plausible theory was offered according to which such a statement is equivalent to a cheer or a boo, which expresses a feeling. What I might call value-scepticism has thus been an axiological problem. I will add that anyone who says that value judgements are meaningless believes not only that this is true but that it is worth saying, which is a value judgement.

[1] Russell, *Religion and Science*, p. 230.

Another axiological problem is whether all or only some values are purely subjective. The Neo-Scholastic philosophers affirm that, like unity and truth, goodness is one of what they call the transcendental properties of being[2] and since being is primarily objective this amounts to an affirmation of the objectivity of at least the main values. As for the Personalists, in 1897 Scheler said:

> We must abandon the prejudice of thinking that objectivity must be the same for everything. The law of gravity existed long before Newton discovered it. Values have this kind of objectivity: they are independent of all individual opinions and desires. In this way values can be considered no less objective than physical objects.[3]

A third axiological problem is: what is the primary value? Commonly, when people propose value-theories they maintain that something is of primary value and that all other values are derived from it. For instance, some recent thinkers maintain that evolution has primary value and that things have value or disvalue in so far as they aid or impede it. Centuries ago, Ignatius Loyola maintained, not in these words, that the praise, reverence and service of God and the salvation of the soul are of primary value, and all other things have value or disvalue in so far as they contribute to this or impede it. His "first principle and foundation" was an axiological theory. Ethical systems usually differ from one another in this, that they propose different primary values.

The Scholastic theory
The value of being and the primary value
The Neo-Scholastics had a value-theory, which they expressed using the word "good". Their basic thesis was: the primary value is that of *being*. This meant that something is good in so far as it is a being, and only in that way, and the more perfect we are as beings the better we are.

Value is in the whole
It is, of course, generally believed that when a single being has parts, value resides in the whole, not in the parts taken by themselves. The

---

2 See above, p. 91.
3 Scheler, *Beiträge*, p. 83; quoted in Staude, *Max Scheler*, p. 16.

Scholastics did not maintain that the created universe is a single being of which we are all only parts, but they did maintain that value resides primarily in the universe. For instance, Thomas said: "A particular good is ordered to the good of the whole as a means to an end, or as an imperfect thing to a perfect thing",[4] and he went on to apply that to the universe. He also said, with a reference to Aristotle: "What is best in things is the good of the order of the universe".[5]

Intellectualism

According to the Scholastics, the fundamental reality which makes beings superior to animals, plants and minerals is rationality; this, then, they said, is the source of the peculiar value of human beings. This led them to profess intellectualism, which was formulated as follows by Rousselot:

> I understand by intellectualism the doctrine which places the supreme value and intensity of life in an act of intellect, that sees in this act the radical and essential good, and regards all things else as good only in so far as they participate in it.[6]

For intellectualists, then, love is good in so far as it is rational and if we see that one person loves another we should say, "How rational, *and therefore* how good" or "That person's love will help the acquisition and diffusion of knowledge and understanding, *therefore* it is good". Maritain said that "the superiority of the speculative over the practical intellect", or the superiority of spectator philosophy over agent philosophy, is "an essential thesis of Thomism".[7]

In *Insight* Lonergan presented this vision of life in a clear way. We should, he said, "conceive the good as identical with the intelligibility that is intrinsic to being",[8] and "it will not be amiss to assert emphatically that the identification of being and the good bypasses human feelings and sentiments to take its stand exclusively upon intelligible

---

[4] *"Bonum particulare ordinatur ad bonum totius sicut ad finem, ut imperfectum ad perfectum"* (Thomas, *Summa Contra Gentiles*, I,86).

[5] *"Quod est optimum in rebus existens, est bonum ordinis universi"* (Thomas, *Summa Theologica*, 1 15 2 c).

[6] Rousselot, *The Intellectualism of Saint Thomas*, p. 1.

[7] Maritain, *The Person and the Common Good*, p. 24.

[8] Lonergan, *Insight*, p. 604.

order and rational value".[9] Of communication between human beings he said: "Talking is a basic human art. By it each communicates to others what he knows and, at the same time, provokes the contradictions that direct his attention to what he has overlooked".[10] By speech and example, he said, "there is effected a sustained communication that at once disseminates and tests and improves every advance [in knowledge] to make the achievement of each successive generation the starting-point of the next".[11] For there to be scientific progress, no one can do all the necessary experiments himself; "belief, then, is an essential element in scientific collaboration".[12] Nor is this confined to science: if "man's sensitive nature" did not have to be considered, "social development would be simply a matter of intellectual development".[13]

Inequality or the grades of being

According to Scholasticism, more being or reality has greater value than less. Life, consciousness and rationality are realities and therefore a plant has more value than an anorganic thing, an animal has more value than a plant and a human being has more value than an animal. Moreover, intelligent animals like dogs have more value than unintelligent insects and highly intelligent human beings have more value than stupid ones. Also, in an orchestra some players contribute more than others to the work being played and this means that they have greater value; just so, in the universe those creatures which contribute more to the whole have more value that those which contribute less, and Thomas said that "rational creatures are most principally ordered to the good of the universe",[14] which implies that they have the most value. That is, the scholastics had a strong sense of the inequality of beings and "the grades of being" was such a fundamental feature of Thomas's universe that he used it as the basis of one of his proofs of the existence of God.

[9] Ibid., p. 606.
[10] Ibid., p. 174.
[11] Ibid., p. 175.
[12] Ibid., p. 428.
[13] Ibid., p. 597.
[14] *"Inter autem omnes creaturas, principalius ordinantur ad bonum universi creaturae rationales"* (Thomas, *Summa Theologica*, 1 23 7 c).

The statement that the greatest in any category is the final cause of the inferiors[15] can be put in value-terms: there is a hierarchy of values, and ultimately beings of lesser value exist to serve beings of higher value: animals exist to satisfy the needs of human beings and, among human beings, inferior human beings serve those who are superior to them.

Disvalue

Having said that every being is good, the scholastics were ultimately compelled to maintain that evil is a *privatio* or lack of being, that is, the absence of something which ought to be present. This is sometimes plausible: for instance, blindness is not a positive reality but lack of sight and stupidity is lack of intelligence. It is, however, difficult to explain a rampaging tiger, cancer or the huge illicit-drug industry and the traffic in human beings as non-realities, and it is almost immediately said that we should consider not only particular beings in isolation but the universe as a whole; when we do that, we become aware of *lacks of order* in it, such as exist when a tiger on the rampage kills human beings or when cells in a body grow in a disorderly way and threaten vital organs. That disvalue or evil is lack of *being or order* fits many phenomena. It does not, however, fit moral evil, as I shall later say.

Criticism of the Scholastic value-theory

Neo-Scholastic Intellectualism is unacceptable for several reasons. First, it attributes intrinsic value only to knowledge of being, understood as objective reality: that is, only to fact-finding. This denies value to novels, fantasy, jokes and the words of most songs. Also, the statement that if "man's sensitive nature" did not have to be considered, "social development would be simply a matter of intellectual development" puts charity among those things which have to be considered only because of "man's sensitive nature", which is appalling. Finally, I can imagine Lonergan's words about conversation, quoted above, ringing a bell with architects who are planning a research centre and who take care to provide recreation rooms in which workers in different fields,

---

[15] See above, p. 91.

leaving their laboratories, can mingle, talk about what they are doing, make suggestions to each other and sometimes have their attention drawn to what they have overlooked. That is, the conversations can help them in their research. On the other hand, if a man and a woman have fallen in love and talk to each other for hours, their aim is not to increase each other's fund of information and have attention drawn to what they have overlooked; neither does the statement fit most social conversation. That is, Lonergan's is a highly intellectualist notion of the value of communication, and it is not true of interpersonal communication. Maritain, writing earlier than Lonergan, was slightly more positive: he said that as a person a human being "talks with another person, communicates with him by understanding and affection" in a "dialogue in which souls communicate".[16] However, he said that such communication is rarely possible and he said little about it.

According to Scholasticism, whenever there is question of assessing a particular person's value, we should consider what he or she is *objectively*. This is sometimes true. For instance, if we want a man for a lifting job, we look for one with sufficient physical strength. It is, however, by no means always true, for we often see value in *subjective* factors and when we say that someone is a good person it is his or her subjective qualities which we have most in mind.

Finally, the idea that value resides in wholes rather than in parts taken by themselves is acceptable when it is applied to single beings. It might be acceptable when it is applied to an ensemble of purely material beings, which is why a farmer might shoot a cow for the sake of a herd as a whole. It is not acceptable, however, when applied to human persons.

Personalist value-theory

Most Personalists maintain that the primary value is that of the person and this is where a difference appears between Scholasticism and Personalism. T. H. Green, who died in 1882, said:

> There can be nothing in a nation however exalted its mission, or in a society however perfectly organised, which is not in the persons

---

[16] Maritain, *The Degrees of Knowledge* (1932), p. 231.

composing the nation or the society. Our ultimate standard of worth is an ideal of personal worth. To speak of any progress or improvement of a nation or a society or mankind, except as relative to some greater worth of persons, is to use words without meaning.[17]

A Neo-Scholastic might say that, being rational, a person is the highest kind of being and therefore has the highest worth, but Personalists affirm that persons have value *as persons,* which does not mean the same as *as beings.*

I myself believe that all beings have at least some value as beings so that, for instance, if a tree is destroyed in a bushfire this is bad, whether or not it is precious to any persons, and I believe that human beings have some value because of the kind of beings they are and because of what they contribute to the universe. But, and this is where I disagree with the Scholastics, I maintain that persons have value as persons, over and above the value which they have as beings, and that this is a higher value.

The one and the many in Neo-Scholasticism and Personalism

When the Neo-Scholastics maintained that being is one, true and good, they put "one" with "true" and "good" and by implication they put "many", which starts with two, with "false" and "bad". This meant that **one is good, two is bad, three is worse.** No scholastic philosophers ever said this, of course, but it was implicit in what they did say and it underlay the notion that value is primarily located in the whole universe, which has a certain unity *and so* is good. In Personalist value-theory, on the other hand, every person in his or her individuality has intrinsic value, so that there are as many primary values as there are persons. The Personalist world-picture is thus more granular than that of Neo-Scholasticism. Also, Personalists believe that *the other person* is of immense significance and value in any person's life, and that no person can be happy or fulfilled on his or her own. A hitherto unstated Personalist principle is: **One is bad, two is good, three is better.**

---

[17] Green, *Prologemena to Ethics,* p. 193; quoted above, p. 42.

Chapter 8

Love

Scholastic philosophy

The main theory
In spite of the importance of love in life and in Christianity, Neo-Scholastic philosophy textbooks had only a page or two, or even nothing, about it, and when in the late nineteen-fifties I set out to write a thesis on love I was surprised to find how little had been written about it by Scholastic authors. I can see reasons for this. One was their intellectualism. Another is that they may have been vaguely troubled by the conclusions to which they were led when they applied Neo-Scholastic principles to love, and so avoided the subject.

An underlying principle of Scholastic Philosophy was that ideally subjectivity conforms to objective reality. This led the Scholastics to assume that, to be good, love must correspond to, and by explained by, objective reality. From Aristotle came the idea that the primary love is self-love. In it, the person as subject voluntarily accepts or "affirms" the objective reality which is himself or herself; then there is perfect conformity of the subjectivity to objective reality. It remained to explain love of *other* beings. If I go to a bullfight and enjoy it and if I find that it was a typical bullfight, I say that I enjoy bullfighting and that I am in favour of bullfights in general. Similarly, said the Scholastics, if I love myself as a certain kind of being, I implicitly love all other beings of the same kind, and if I love myelf as a being, I implicitly love all beings. Thus self-love has other-love implicit in it and love between different beings is based on their having something in common in their natures. Scholastics sometimes called this *communicatio*, adding that by this they did not mean people talking to one another, which is what we usually mean by "communication". Joseph M.Keller said:

It is plain that when St Thomas says, "such mutual benevolence is based on some communication", the "communication" formally speaking ought not to be undestood as social intercourse or conversation, but as the likeness that exists between beings by virtue of the fact that they have in common some particular perfection.[1]

Thomas said, "Likeness is the principle of loving".[2] When beings have the same nature they are one in this respect and Rousselot said that "there is no other principle of direct and true love besides unity" and "a thing is loved in so far as it is one with the loving subject".[3] That is, the basis of love is objective, not subjective.

A slightly different theory was proposed by the Scholastics who said that value resides in the whole. They explained love by saying that one wills or loves the whole to which one belongs, and oneself and other human beings as elements of it. Fernand Van Steenberghen, for instance, having said that "every being is desirable or good in so far as it exists", went on to say that my will does not find a distinct joy in every existing thing; rather, he said, "it enjoys the universal order which is known by my intellect in a confused way at least".[4] The universe, according to Van Steenberghen, is like a beautiful melody, which one enjoys as a whole, enjoying every note as it is played but only as an element of the melody—if any note were to be played on its own, it would not be music and one would not enjoy it.

This kind of love is found in families, whose members resemble each other objectively and who all together form a single entity, the family. In the Middle Ages people were aware of families but there was little in the high culture about good sexual love, while at a low level there were bawdy songs. The Neo-Scholastics were mostly clerics, who were to a large extent cut off from the general culture. Until late in the period of Neo-Scholasticism there was no radio or television and clerics, especially students, did not listen to recorded love-songs or read love

---

[1] Keller, "De virtute caritatis ut amicitia quadam divina" (1925), p. 251. The same was said by Simonin in "Autour de la solution thomiste du problème de l'amour" (1931), p. 265 and by Gillon in "A propos de la théorie thomiste de l'amitié" (1948), p. 15.
[2] *"Similitudo est principium amandi"* (Thomas, *Summa Theologica*, 1 7 4 ad 2).
[3] Rousselot, *The Problem of Love*, pp. 87-89.
[4] Van Steenberghen, *Ontology*, p. 63.

stories. Also, in many serious writings about religious life, the term "particular friendship" was a euphemism for a homosexual attachment between two members of a community. A particular friendship in this sense was characterised by exclusiveness and emotional intensity. Unfortunately, these writings led many religious to regard friendships between particular persons as undesirable. On the other hand, they did experience family-love, the camaraderie of students and, later, that of priests, and the "fraternal charity" of members of religious orders. The theory of love which I have just outlined, therefore, fitted their experience of love and systematised their ideas about it

This love is also found in countries, the citizens of which often share certain characteristics and together form a single whole, the nation to which they belong.

Some secondary ideas

The scholastic view that causes are superior to their effects, or that if one thing flows from another it is inferior to it,[5] implied that, since love of other beings flows from self-love, self-love is the greatest love. This led Thomas to say that a person is obliged in charity to love himself more than his neighbour.[6] I suspect that this is one of the ideas that Neo-Scholastic philosophers were uneasy about.

It follows from the theory above that the more I have in common with someone else, the greater is my love for him or her. That is, loves are subjectively unequal, *for objective reasons.* This is similar to what some contemporary sociobiologists say, that we are genetically programed to be generous to other people to an extent that is determined by how many genes we share with them. Also, if the primary object of love is the whole, loves are unequal for objective reasons, since some beings belong more to the whole (for instance, relatives in a family can be close or distant), or contribute more to it, than others.

Dominance

Some Scholastics applied to love the Thomist principle that when beings are united it is as act and potency: in love, they said, beings

---

[5] See above, p. 91.
[6] *"Homo ex caritate magis debet diligere seipsum quam proximum"* (Thomas, *Summa Theologica*, 2-2 26 4 sed contra).

are united, hence they must be to one another as act and potency, determinant and determined. In a passage which I quoted earlier, Rousselot said:

> This is a principle of St Thomas's metaphysics: each time two beings unite so as to form an assemblage that is truly unified [*un*], the relations between the two constituents are those of the determinant and the determined; one is as it were the matter and the other the form.

He applied this to love and dismissed love between equals in these terms: "The worst position to take in order to construct a metaphysics of love is precisely to look at things from the vantage point of egalitarian friendship".[7] The ideal married couple, in this scheme of things, consists of a man dominating a woman and a woman agreeing with everything the man says and letting him make all the decisions, so that there is in effect only one mind and will, his. In such a pair the man is the form, the woman is matter, and they form a united couple. If Rousselot saw a couple or two friends each of whom had a mind and will of his or her own, and neither of whom dominated the other, he judged them to be united in a loose and inferior way, if at all. He actually said: "Perfectly egalitarian friendship is not desirable, is not possible, does not exist".[8]

Finally, as we have seen, in their intellectualist hierarchy of values scholastics rated intellectual above volitional activity and hence knowledge above love.

Personalists and love

Since they studied the "phenomena" of subjectivity, the Personalists wrote a good deal about love. For instance, Scheler wrote *The Nature of Sympathy* in 1913 and Maurice Nédoncelle wrote *Vers une philosophie de l'amour* in 1946.[9] Of course, they said that one loves persons as persons. If we talk about people as human beings, our attention is on

---

[7] Rousselot, *The Problem of Love*, p. 113. See above, p. 88.
[8] Ibid.
[9] Scheler's book was first called *Towards the Phenomenology of the Sympathy Feelings of Love and Hate*, then the title was changed to *The Nature and Forms of Sympathy*. Nédoncelle's book was later enlarged and entitled *Vers une phiosophie de l'amour et de la personne*.

what they have in common; but as persons they are distinct individuals, so that for me to love another as a person is necessarily to love him or her not as another version of myself to whom my self-love naturally extends but as an *other* person, not me but someone else.

In love, then, two persons feel distinct from one another, they are profoundly aware of the fact that there are two of them, and they find this delightful. Scott Peck says:

> A major characteristic of genuine love is that the distinction between oneself and the other is always maintained and preserved. The genuine lover always perceives the beloved as someone who has a totally separate identity. Moreover, the genuine lover always respects and even encourages this separateness and the unique individuality of the beloved.[10]

Erich Fromm puts the matter succinctly: "In love the paradox occurs that two beings become one and yet remain two".[11] In Personalist Philosophy, two is good, so love keeps the two.

Also, as persons people are subjects and it is as subjects that they love one another. They may have something objective in common, and indeed they need to have something in common to be able to communicate, but this is not the basis of their relationship.

To say that someone is loved as a subject does not mean that he or she is loved as a purely spiritual consciousness, because there is a subjectivity of the body as well as of the intellect and, obviously, this is of enormous importance in sexual love.

One feature of this kind of love is that it exists between equals. By this I do not mean that to become friends two persons must be of the same age and of equal intelligence or wealth; I mean that in their relationship neither of them looks up to or down on the other. If, for instance, two teachers and their wives are friends and one of them is made the principal, they can remain friends, provided that when they meet socially they regard each other as equals, even though at the school one of them has authority over the other. Rousselot was

---

[10] Peck, *The Road Less Traveled*, pp 160-161. I would not use the word "separate" here, since it often implies physical distance, as when we say that in some refugee camps husbands and wives are separated, and it sometimes implies a breach in a relationship, as when we say that a husband and wife have separated. "Distinct" does not have either of these connotations.

[11] Fromm, *The Art of Loving*, p. 21.

hopelessly wrong about this. His mistake consisted in applying to the phenomena of subjectivity "a principle of the metaphysics of St Thomas" which is valid only of beings as objects. He did not realise that subjectivity has a life of its own.

A view which combines both theories

I maintain that there are basically two different kinds of love.[12] In one kind, an objective link is prior to the love and is the reason for it. For instance, two siblings are linked and love each other by virtue of the fact that they have the same parents. Also, in submarine crews and in some sporting teams a quite intense "camaraderie" develops which is a form of love, and it is based on the common belonging to the group. In this love, people are not loved precisely as persons. In the other kind of love, the species of which are sexual love and friendship, persons meet as subjects, commit themselves to each other as persons and so create the union that comes to exist between them. The second of these loves is higher than the first kind, as person is higher than being.

Two persons can love each other in both ways at once, and this is common. For instance, in a large family it is possible for two siblings to love each other as they love all their brothers and sisters and, in addition, to be friends with one another as neither is with any of the others. It is possible for two members of a religious order to love each other with both "fraternal charity" and friendship; in this case, if one of them leaves the order they will no longer share in the love which all its member have for one another but they may remain friends, while if they both remain in the order but are separated for a long time their friendship may die, so that if they meet again it is as people who once were friends, but they may feel that membership of the order is a bond of love between them.

---

[12] Cowburn, *Love*. What is said above is a summary of the main thesis of this book.

Chapter 9

Ethics

Scholasticism

In general

Scholastic Philosophy dealt with the natures of beings and their causes rather than human behaviour but, particularly in the time of Neo-Scholasticism, when most of the students were priests-to-be, the need was felt to deal in the philosophy course with ethical issues about which unacceptable ideas were circulating: these included divorce, private property, socialism and democracy. Also, much of the reasoning of moral theologians is philosophical and a vast literature has come into existence in which one does not find characteristic Scholastic terms like potency and act, matter and form, essence and existence or substance and accident. When, then, people say that Neo-Scholasticism is dead, they are not talking about the work which was done and is being done in the Catholic Church on ethics and moral theology. However, a basic Scholastic idea is that just as truth is the conformity of the *intellect* to being, so moral goodness is the conformity of the *will* to being. An act of the will is declared to be morally good when it issues in actions which aim to attain objective or natural purposes, morally bad when it is in conflict with these, and morally neutral when it is not aimed at attaining them but is not in conflict with them, either. While subjective factors like knowledge and the degree of responsibility were considered when there was question of the innocence or guilt of people who had freely done particular things, there was a tendency to underrate the significance of subjective experience when discussing this or that action, in general.

Sexual morality

In their discussion of sexual morality the Scholastic philosophers began by considering sexual intercourse objectively, as a physical action, and they said that its natural purpose (or *finis operis*) is to bring about conception and ultimately the birth of a child; children, they went on to say, need the care of a mother and father together; therefore, they concluded, sexual intercourse is morally good only when the partners are a man and a woman who are committed to living together, bringing up their children, for life, *primarily because this is what is needed for the procreation and upbringing of children.* They did say that marriage has a secondary end, the happiness and fulfilment of the couple; this was the *finis operantis* or the purpose of the agent, and it was subjective. Primacy was thus clearly given to the objective over the subjective. According to this view, adultery is immoral *primarily* because it endangers the children; that it wrecks the interpersonal relationship between the spouses and is a betrayal of their love is *secondary.* They maintained, then, that if a husband and wife engage in foreplay for a considerable time before they have intercourse, this is morally good because it and the intercourse, taken together, make up the love-making the natural purpose of which is conception. They also said that it is not immoral for couples to have intercourse when they know that it will not lead to conception.

Ownership

In their discussion of the morality of ownership and the immorality of theft, scholastic philosophers began from the objective fact that human beings need material things not all of which are freely available in the way that air is. Being rational beings, they said, human beings need to make provision for their futures and therefore, either individually or in communities, they need to own some things, which it would be wrong for others to damage or take from them. In particular, parents of children need to have possessions in order to provide for them.

Socio-political issues

Scholastic philosophers were highly conscious of inequality and this affected their thinking about how society should be organised. I quoted

Rousselot's statement that whenever two unite to form an ensemble which is truly one, the relation of the two to each other is that of determinant and determined; one is as it were the form and the other is the matter.[1] In the political area, this means that ideally when millions of men and women form one nation there is one person at the top, who is the form, and below him or her there is the mass of people, who are the matter. Sometimes between the monarch and the more or less vulgar mob there is a ruling class of superior persons, who on the one hand accept their inferior position vis-à-vis the monarch and on the other hand insist on their superiority to the common people. The Scholastic view that the less good being exists for the better one could be taken as implying that it was right for working-class people to be treated as if their purpose in life was to serve higher-class people—the whole purpose in life of the people downstairs was to make possible the kind of life enjoyed by the people upstairs. It is not surprising that leading French Neo-Scholastic philosophers such as Louis Billot SJ and Réginald Garrigou-Lagrange OP, who were Thomists, and Pedro Descoqs SJ, who was a Suarezian, were strong supporters of the *Action Française*, which was a fiercely anti-democratic political movement.[2] However, in the time of Neo-Scholasticism the Church frequently sided with the workers. For instance, in a time of depression Leo XIII issued *Rerum Novarum* and in the time of another depression Pius XI issued *Quadragesimo Anno*.

Personalism
A Personalist criticism of Neo-Scholastic ethics

Most people surely find the ethical theory which I have just expounded objectionable, not to say repulsive, particularly because so little attention is given to subjective experience and there is so little appreciation of the value of persons as persons. People react in this way because of the pervasive influence of Personalism and, as I said earlier, the ethics of the Catholic Church today is explicitly Personalist. Not that Catholic

---

[1] See above, p. 88.
[2] In 1927 Pius XI condemned Maurras, the leader of the *Action Française*. Billot, who turned eighty-one in that year, manifested support or at least sympathy for him, whereupon the pope deposed him as a cardinal.

Personalists deny objective reality or have an entirely subjective approach to ethics: the point is that they have subjective thoughts and feelings at the forefront of their minds.

Regarding sexual ethics, first, it seems to me that in reality there was almost always a divergence between the theory of the primary and secondary ends of marriage, and the subjective thinking and willing of couples. Almost no couples getting married regarded the having and upbringing of children as the *primary* purpose of their marriage. For them, the primary purpose was what was called a secondary purpose of marriage.

Also, it seems to me that if teachers who desired to communicate to teenagers some understanding of mature sexual experience were to tell them the physical facts, with anatomical diagrams, and were to describe sexual intercourse as a physical activity, and that was all, they would fail miserably. If, on the other hand, they were try to communicate to the teenagers what it feels like for a mature man and woman to be in love with each other, and how by making love they give themselves to each other so that it is primarily to express their love that they engage in it: that is, if they were to convey an understanding of lovemaking as a subjective, highly personal experience and if, when they had finished, the teenagers were to have an understanding of why what is physically the same action is wonderful when the couple are in love, meaningless when they are not, and horrible when it is rape, they would have given them some understanding of human sexuality. If they wished to go on and deal with sexual morality, they would have established a basis for it. Similarly, ethicists and moral theologians should derive sexual morality, primarily (not exclusively) from the subjective experience of sexual love. They should appreciate the fact that when people express their love for each other by kissing and other actions besides sexual intercourse, these actions are positively good not merely because they are preludes to intercourse but because of the love which is expressed in them. In *Love and Responsibility* John Paul II, then Karol Wojtyla, set out to do precisely this.

Ownership is often important because of practical, objective considerations, but it is often more important because of what things mean to owners in their subjectivities. Suppose, for instance, that an old man in a nursing home has a useless vase which his dead wife made for him on his fiftieth birthday and other souvenirs of his past life, and photographs and presents from grandchildren which represent the future which he himself will not live to see but the thought of which delights him; objectively, these things might be of no practical use and when he dies they might be thrown out; but they have immense value to him as a person and from this comes the obligation of the people who look after him to take good care of them. Also, if a woman comes home and finds that a burglar, probably a man, has been in her house, rummaging in her cupboards and looking through her underclothes for hidden jewels, she may well feel that she has been molested and this, which is subjective, may be more deeply experienced by her than the loss of a DVD player. The moral laws concerning ownership, therefore, should be derived not only from a consideration of objective usefulness but also, and sometimes primarily, from reflection on the way persons embody themselves in material things, which may or may not be useful. As Mounier said, "human ownership is personal ownership".[3]

In socio-political issues, there is today an awareness of people's equality as persons, which exists when, as is usually the case, they are unequal in intelligence and ability. Not so long ago, when couples got married the woman promised to obey the man, so that inequality was expressed in the vows; these words are now omitted and it is as equals that they marry. When adult brothers and sisters, whose father has died, meet to decide some family matter, as a rule it is no longer assumed that the eldest son is the head of the family and that, after listening to the others, he will make the decisions; votes are taken and they are all of equal value. In democracies, too, all votes are of equal value. In all this one can see a belief in the equality of persons as persons, which comes naturally to everyone who has been influenced by Personalism.

Moral evil

The scholastic view that evil is a lack of being is plausible where undesirable physical phenomena which are no one's fault are concerned, especially if "lack of being" is extended to include lack of order. Such

---

[3] Mounier, "From Capitalist Property to Personal Property" (1934), *Oeuvres*, I, 34.

things may be bad but they are not, properly speaking, evil. If a man does not love his wife and so does not care whether she is happy or not, this is bad but it is not *evil,* as hate, which would consist in positively wanting her to be unahppy, would be. Also, it would be wrong to say that there is nothing positive in adultery, it is is just lack of fidelity. More generally, immorality is not the absence of moral goodness from human behaviour. Also, the Scholastics maintained that one can no more will what one knows to be bad than one can believe what one knows to be false, but in moral evil persons choose evil knowing it to be evil.

Part III

Theology

Chapter 10

Scholasticism and Personalism in Theology

In this book I have from time to time mentioned religious matters, if only because Scholastic Philosophy was almost entirely a Catholic clerical enterprise, but I shall now deal directly with them.

I have said that Scholastic Philosophy was a study of *ens in quantum ens* or being as being, and Scholastic Theology was what has been called "perfect-being theology".[1] When theologians were influenced by Personalism, however, their main interest was the person.

The person in theology

I once heard a distinguished English Scholastic philosopher, a Catholic priest, say that "person" is a purely theological term which should not be defined in philosophy (any more than philosophers define a sacrament). As I said earlier, most scholastic philosophers gave a definition of the term, which they explained, but, having done that, they did not mention it again.[2] For instance, if they offered a theory of love it was not a love of persons as such, and in their ethics they talked about human nature, not human persons. In theology, the Scholastic theologians talked about the divine persons when they were discussing the Trinity, and they talked about the Second Person when they were discussing the Incarnation, but elsewhere they did not talk either about the divine persons or about human persons. Wojtyla said that in theology "we encounter the word 'person' in the treatises on Trinity and Incarnation, but it is hardly to be found in works on man". He

---

[1] See Thomas V. Morris of Notre Dame University, "Perfect Being Theology".
[2] See above, p. 93.

meant that the word was rarely used in theological works about human beings, such as the treatise on grace, of which Rahner said that it was "monotheistic, not trinitarian".³ He meant "unitarian". I will say later how they justified this.

In Oxford in 1890, a theological book, *Lux Mundi,* was published in which R. L. Ottley said that "God is an Infinite, but Personal Being", who is "willing to become the centre of a realm of personalities" and who to this end "called into existence a world of personal beings, in a sense independent of Himself". He said that Christianity "lays stress on the principle of *personality*" and that, for a Christian, "religion consists in personal relations between man and God".⁴ In 1912-13, in Scotland, Andrew Seth Pringle-Pattison insisted on the importance which Christianity attributes to individual persons. He said:

> The essential feature of the Christian conception of the world, in contrast to the Hellenic, may be said to be that it regards the person and the relations of persons to one another as the essence of reality, whereas Greek thought conceived of personality, however spiritual, as a restrictive characteristic of the finite—a transitory product of a life which as a whole is impersonal.⁵

He said: "I have a centre of my own—a will of my own—which no one shares with me or can share—a centre which I maintain even in my dealings with God Himself." ⁶ In saying this, he was denying pantheism, and in particular the Hegelianism of his time. Other non-Catholics wrote in a similar way about how, as Kierkegaard had said, Christianity is *personal*.

At an earlier time a sign of life in the Catholic Church was the appearance of new religious orders. In the twentieth century some new orders appeared but also what were called movements appeared, which turned out to be more significant. Notable among these were the biblical movement, Catholic Action, the liturgical movement and the ecumenical movement. These brought together people of

---

³ Rahner, *The Trinity*, p. 123.
⁴ Ottley, "Christian Ethics", pp. 469, 471. We do not use the word "personality" as Ottley used it.
⁵ Seth Pringle-Pattison, *The Idea of God in the Light of Recent Philosophy*, p. 291.
⁶ Seth Pringle-Pattison, *Hegelianism and Personality*, p. 217.

different countries, religious of different orders, diocesan bishops and priests, brothers, nuns and laypeople. They did not involve vows and full-time commitment, they were open to men and women, and they were not regulated by canon law as religious orders were. The people in these movements experienced joyful camaraderie and tremendous hopefulness. "The Church," they felt, "is alive and well and we are transforming it." At Vatican II the assembled bishops of the Church granted to these movements almost everything they had been asking for and the transformation was sped up. I said earlier that, generally speaking, the members of these movements did not profess Personalism, but respect for all persons was important to all of them and at Vatican II this became apparent.

Most of the post-conciliar developments in Church life and especially in religious orders were bewildering to people who had not been affected by Personalism but they were understood and welcomed by those whose thinking had been influenced by it, whether they had heard of it under that name or not. This is because what were called "the changes in the Church" were made not for practical reasons such as "to attract young people" but as elements of a Personalist revolution. Mounier may have failed to bring about a "personalist and communitarian revolution" in France, but his followers succeeded in bringing one about in the Catholic Church.

Theology in general
How a Christian begins intellectually:
the first phase: believing what is in the Bible

Christian theology begins with the intellectual acceptance by Christians of the Bible as the inspired word of God.

The medieval Scholastics read or heard the Bible in their divine office and Mass, during which time their approach was "spiritual", which is to say that their critical faculties were at rest. Few of them knew any Hebrew or Greek and they used a Latin translation all the time; also, they knew no more about the Jewish culture than is revealed in the Bible itself. They believed that the various authors to whom the books of the Bible are attributed were inspired, and they tended to take the books as being primarily "the word of the Lord" and only secondarily the work of human beings, so they were not particularly interested in looking for differences between the various human authors. Also, for the most part in the books of the Bible the terms used are not defined, nothing is systematically explained and chapters are not in logical order such as one might find in a modern book called *The Teaching of the Catholic Church*. In their scholarly work, the Scholastics were highly systematic, so that the Bible could not have been easy for them to use in their lectures.

Like the medieval Scholastics, the Neo-Scholastic philosophers and theologians read the Bible daily in the divine office and at Mass, and they meditated on gospel passages. In their lectures and books they quoted texts from the Bible, and a course of theology included subjects such as *Introduction to the Old Testament, Introduction to the New Testament,* and *Exegesis,* in which selected texts were studied in detail. However, from a present-day point of view they were extremely ignorant of when and how the books of the Bible were written and how they were originally understood. In their main courses, which were on topics such as *God as One, The Trinity, the Incarnation, The Church* and so on, they briefly quoted selected texts, usually not situating them in their contexts, and then got down to business. Billot was perhaps extreme in being almost contemptuous of the Bible when he was speaking as a professor of theology, but the others were not much better.

In the nineteenth century men appeared in the Church who had a scholarly as distinct from a purely spiritual approach to the Bible. Then, unfortunately, came the Modernist crisis[7] and for a time this Biblical movement was stopped. Many of the men who were in it put aside what they had been working on and devoted themselves to work on ancient languages or to parish work. However, the movement went on in a semi-underground fashion and it grew stronger and gradually more visible until at last, in 1943, Pius XII issued the encyclical *Divino Afflante Spiritu,* which gave it a green light and after World War II scripture scholars became perhaps the most influential people in Catholic scholarly circles so that at Vatican II, which was held about twenty years after *Divino Afflante Spiritu,* a need was felt for more scripure in the liturgy and in the training of priests, and for the use of "biblical language" in the decrees of the council itself. Now, at the

---

[7] See above, p. 37-38.

Chapter 10: *Personalism & Scholasticism in Theology* 139

time at which I am writing, about forty years later, all future priests devote much time to study of the Bible and a typical contemporary book on the Trinity, for instance, devotes many pages to it.

Many scripture scholars are like a man who studies the ancient Greek games. He studies statues, pictures on pots and archaeological remains and he endeavours to form what I might call an overview of the games. If he is successful, he finally produces a book in which he has chapters in logical order on the training, the rules, the prizes, the rituals, the judges, the spectators and perhaps the treatment of injuries. In a somewhat analogous way, a scripture scholar may take all the references to the Holy Spirit (for instance) which he can find, and try to combine then into a general picture of what the Holy Spirit was to the people of the time when the books of the New Testament were written.

That there should be a second phase

Some lecturers, it seems to me, present the Biblical teaching and then stop. Also, some preachers at Mass explain the passages from the Bible which have just been read and then step down. It seems to me that we Christians need not only to know what the scriptures meant to their first readers but to understand the beliefs which we have now, usually in terms of our own culture. For instance, the early Christians believed in a flat earth, with the heavens above it and an underworld below it, and we need to re-think the passages in which this picture is assumed. I said that a classical scholar might produce a book about the ancient Greek games *as they were played and watched at the time.* Someone else might say that sport should be played and watched now in the spirit of ancient Greece, and, using that book, he might write a book about modern sport *as it ought to be played and watched now.* His book would be a little analogous to the works of contemporary theologians.

Other lecturers, authors and preachers do not present the Biblical teaching and then stop, but they go on at length about the Bible and then at the end they devote a few minutes or a few pages to how we ought now to understand what we believe. This seems to me to be going from one extreme to the other: from almost no Bible to almost nothing but the Bible.

Using a philosophy

Understanding something usually consists in setting it in a general picture, and often Christians have found certain philosophies helpful, precisely because they were general ideas of reality. As I said earlier, they have usually not found low philosophies in any way helpful but they have been impressed by high philosophies which included beliefs in other-worldly beings and which had high ethical ideals.[8] There is then talk of Philosophical Theology.

Often when a philosophy which is not the work of a Christian is used by a Christian in the search for understanding of his beliefs, there are things in it which conflict with Christian teaching. At this point the person may opt for the philosophy and simply abandon Christianity. Alternatively, he may declare that our understanding of the Christian teaching must be changed to bring it into accord with the philosophy. It is in this way that heresies sometimes come into existence. Ideally, the Christian rejects whatever in the philosophy does not accord with Christian teaching. For instance, when Christians used Plato they rejected his idea that human souls exist in a higher realm from which they descend into our world, and when Thomas and others used Aristotle they rejected his idea that love between the divine being and human beings is impossible.

When a pagan philosophy is used by Christian thinkers, even when certain doctrines are rejected there often remains a certain bias so that the Christian teaching, while it is not denied, is distorted. For instance, the Christians who used Neo-Platonism were often so impressed by its unworldliness that they were inclined to underestimate the importance of the human body and the value of material things.

The use of philosophy in the past

Before his conversion, Augustine had been a professional philosopher and when he became a Christian he found an affinity between his Christian beliefs and Plotinus's Neo-Platonism. As I said earlier, he wrote in Latin and his books, which survived, were of immense influence for centuries.

As I also said, in the Middle Ages there was a highly systematic search for *understanding* of Christian beliefs. Scholastic Philosophy

---

[8] See above, p. 22.

appeared, which was derived from the ancient Greek philosophies, and it proved in many cases to offer a way of doing this. For instance, the gospels do not use the term "transubstantiation", but in the twelfth century it was found that this term can be used to explain what Jesus meant when he said, "This is my body" and in 1215 the fourth Lateran Council used it in a statement of belief.

In the Modern Age some Catholics used Descartes's philosophy to enable them, they thought, to understand Catholic beliefs. Others used other philosophies.

When the Neo-Scholastics came on the scene in the nineteenth century, they seem to have believed that in the Bible there were scattered statements, after which there were gropings for understanding of them. Then came the Scholastics, especially Thomas Aquinas, about whom Leo XIII said that he towered over all the other Scholastics and that "faith could scarcely expect more or stronger aids from reason than those which she has already obtained through Thomas".[9] Kleutgen and other early Neo-Scholastics maintained not only that Scholastic Philosophy was true but that it was the only philosophy which could be used to explain Christian doctrines. It was mainly for this reason that Church authorities imposed it.

Using a philosophy now

There has been some recent praise of Thomas as a theologian. For instance, the rules for the training of priests-to-be, issued in 1970, said that in theology students "should regard St Thomas as one of the Church's greatest teachers" (# 86) and in *Fides et Ratio* John Paul II said that "the Church has been justified in consistently proposing Saint Thomas as a master of thought" (# 43). But when *La nouvelle théologie* appeared in the nineteen-forties, what was *nouvelle* about it was, at least partly, that it was not scholastic and generally speaking theology lecturers no longer explain doctrines in terms of act and potency, and if they were to attempt to do so the students would not know what they were talking about.

Some Catholic thinkers were impressed by Existentialism when it appeared after World War II, and they sought to produce a Christian Existentialism. Karl Rahner said that "the Transcendental Method finds

---

[9] Leo XIII, *Aeterni Patris,* # 18.

its deepest meaning in theology" and that "because of the reception of the transcendental method in Catholic philosophy a similar turn is taking *place in theology, so much so that it can no longer be called neo-scholastic in the historical sense*"[10] but the Transcendental Method has not caught on. I can imagine someone reading Jung, not very thoroughly, and conceiving the idea of creating what I might call a Jungian Christianity; but I hope that this will not happen.

One might expect John Paul II to have urged that Personalism replace Scholasticism as the philosophy of the Catholic Church, but he has not done this and neither will I. As I said earlier, in *Fides et Ratio* he said that "the Church has no philosophy of her own nor does she canonise one particular philosophy in preference to others" (# 49). What I propose here is that theologians proceed as they have been doing, not using a philosophy which has a name but offering explanations of Christian beliefs which fit the best views of contemporary men and women. These include:

(1) scientific discoveries, including evolution and what is now known about primitive human beings. A way will have to be found to explain original sin without attributing to an original human couple the power to commit serious sin. Also, when Jesus said that "in the beginning" human beings were monogamous, this will have to be explained. Finally, it is possible that the discovery of indeterminacy in physics, and the role of chance in particle physics and the reproduction of living beings, will make it necessary for theologians to explain divine providence in a new and different way.

(2) social ideas, for instance of racial and sexual equality.

(3) political ideas. It was customary to explain Christ as the king and to represent heaven in paintings as a monarch's court, but it is now generally believed that in general—there is much disagreement about particulars—democracy is the best political system, not only because it works but because of the principles on which it is based.

(4) finally, personalist ideas. While not many people have heard of Personalism, its fundamental idea has taken root in our culture.

---

[10] Rahner, Foreword to Muck, *The Transcendental Method*, p. 10.

Systematic theology and religious spirituality

I distinguished earlier between spectator and agent philosophies and virtually the same distinction can be observed in religious thought. There is systematic theology, which aimed to get knowledge and understanding of Christian truths into people's *heads*. There is also spirituality, which involves exercises that are designed to get a truly Christian spirit into *hearts*. Particularly in the past, if a Catholic professor of systematic theology lectured on the eucharist, he set out to explain how bread and wine become the body and blood of Christ; a "spiritual" book on the same subject told the reader how to prepare to receive communion, how to experience the reception of it and how to make thanksgiving afterwards. Whereas a Catholic course in systematic theology was made up of courses on The Trinity, The Church, The Sacraments and so on, a book of spirituality had chapters on conformity to the will of God, humility, fraternal charity and other subjective experiences.

Systematic theology had its classics, including the speculative writings of the Fathers of the Church and the *Summa Theologica* of Thomas Aquinas, and spirituality had its own classics, from the writings of the desert fathers, the conferences of John Cassian (around AD 400), *The Imitation of Christ* by Thomas A Kempis (fifteenth century), the *Spiritual Exercises* of Ignatius Loyola (sixteenth century), the writings of mystics such as Teresa of Avila and John of the Cross (also sixteenth century), the writings of Francis de Sales (seventeenth century) and others. There were also secondary classics such as *The Practice of Perfection and Christian Virtue* by Alphonsus Rodriguez (1609).

A large religious order of priests had professors of philosophy and theology, who taught many students at a time, in classrooms, only occasionally meeting them individually. It also had "spiritual fathers", who gave talks in chapels and had regular one-to-one meetings with their charges. Often the professors of theology and the spiritual fathers had little to do with one another and the books in their rooms were different. Also, a typical seminary or religious house of study had a theological library, with the books and periodicals to which the professors of theology referred, which the students read for academic purposes and which they were told were not to be used for "spiritual reading"; there was also a library containing books for spiritual reading.

In diocesan seminaries, a seminarian was taught philosophy and spirituality, separately, for two or three years, then he started theology. In the Society of Jesus, a man was a novice and "scholastic" for about eleven years and *then* he began to study theology. The assumption clearly was that theology was a purely intellectual enterprise which had nothing to do with life, the province of spirituality.

A certain rivalry often existed between theology and spirituality. As we have seen, an essential thesis of the Thomism professed by professors of theology used to be that thought is superior to emotion and action.[11] which implied that what professors of theology were doing was superior to what the spirituals were doing. On the other hand, the spirituals could tell each other that Christianity is not in the first place a *Weltbild* or theory of the world, which is meant to be known and understood. It includes a world-picture but to be mistaken does not make anyone an inferior Christian, and while more understanding might make someone a better scientist or philosopher, a Christian who penetrates all mysteries and obtains all knowledge but is without love, is nothing (1 Cor 1:32). This implied that spirituals could feel superior, as Christians, to systematic theologians.

This division has perhaps not entirely disappeared but there is certainly less of a gulf between theology and spirituality. I remember around 1957, which as I write this was almost fifty years ago, leaving a theological lecture which had been given by Karl Rahner and a fellow-student walking beside me said: "We have just heard a long sermon". He was right. It had been both a theological lecture and, because it was going to affect our lives, a sermon. In the kind of theology which Rahner represented, theology and spirituality were not poles apart.

I have been talking about *religious* spiritualities because, whereas the word "spirituality" used to be used in religious circles only, it is now being applied to what I might call noble philosophies of life which are purely secular.

---

[11] See above, p. 115.

Conclusion

I am not going to present complete theological treatises on any of the topics with which I shall deal. In each case, I shall enter the discussion at the point where, having studied the scriptures and the Fathers of the Church, theologians face the search for a contemporary understanding of our faith, and I shall be concerned only with Neo-Scholasticism and Personalism, and the differences between them.

My principal criticism of Neo-Scholastic theology will be that it dealt with God and human beings as beings rather than as persons, stressing objective reality and not sufficiently considering subjective, which is to say properly personal, experience. This is why there was such a gulf between systematic theology and spirituality, one result of which was that spirituality was not sufficiently rational and another was that theology was remote from life. I shall not maintain that the Neo-Scholastics denied that there is such a thing as subjectivity, any more than I shall say that Personalists are subjectivists who deny objective reality. It will be a question of emphasis.

Chapter 11

The Trinity

The doctrine

There are many short references to the Father, the Son and the Spirit in the New Testament but there is no general explanation of how the Father, the Son and the Holy Spirit are both united and distinguished. Here more than elsewhere we find ourselves in the situation analogous to that which I described above, of the person who has many pictures of Greek athletes and wants to understand the games of ancient Greece.

In the early centuries of the Church's existence thinkers endeavoured to form a general picture. Some said that when we talk of the Creator, the Redeemer and the Sanctifier we are really talking about the same person, who has three different roles—this person is like a human being who, we say, at different times wears different hats. This is known as Sabellianism and was condemned in the third century. On the other hand, no one said that there are three Gods. It was, then, understood in the Church that the Father, the Son and the Holy Spirit are really distinct from one another and yet there is one God, but various words were used, in different senses, for what there are three of and what there is one of. In the fourth century there were councils in Nicaea (325) and Constantinople (381), which issued creeds in Greek, but we still have trouble translating them.[1] Eventually, in Latin the words *persona* and *natura* were accepted, they passed almost unchanged into modern languages. It was and is believed that the second person proceeds from, or is generated by, the first person, and the third person

---

[1] The Nicene Creed says that the Son is *homoousios* with the Father. In the Profession of Faith which is used at Mass now this is translated as "one in being with the Father" and Gerald O'Collins translates it as "of the same essence/substance as the Father" (*The Tripersonal God*, p. 115).

proceeds from, or is spirated by, the first two. There is thus one being and one nature and there are two processions and three persons.

There is now talk of the immanent Trinity and the economic Trinity. By the immanent Trinity is meant the three divine persons in their inner life. By the economic Trinity is meant the three divine persons in the activities which produce results outside them.

When the Scholastics said that being is one, true and good, and implicitly put many, which begins with two, with false and bad,[2] they made it difficult for themselves to affirm that in God there are two processions and three persons. They made these affirmations but they were happier when they were talking about *the one God* than when talking about *the three divine persons*. The Thomists maintained that the essence or nature of God is existence, so that in God, and only in God, essence-or-nature and existence are identical. If they had said, therefore, that every divine person has his own existence, distinct from the existences of the others, they would have implied that there are three Gods. They avoided this by saying that while there is one existence which they possess in common, each divine person has his own *subsistence*.[3]

Thomas Aquinas introduced another element into the idea of divine person. He said that in God relation and person are the same, so that the divine persons are "subsistent relations".[4] This made it possible to solve the problem: absolute (as opposed to relative) terms like "substance" and "existence" belong to the one divine nature, while relative terms like "Father" and "Son" belong to the persons.

As Personalists hold that person is higher than being and as they also believe that in the realm of persons one is bad, two is good and three is better,[5] they do not feel that the doctrine of the Trinity is foreign to their system. Instead, they welcome it and feel at home with it. That life at its highest is not solitary but that for each of the highest persons there are other persons, so that the highest life is communitarian, seems to them to be right. Also, the doctrine implies that when we unite

---

[2] See above, p. 119.
[3] See above, p. 94.
[4] In the *Summa Theologica* Thomas maintains that in God "*relatio est idem quod persona*" (1 40 1). He also says: "*"Personae sunt ipsae relationes subsistentes"* (1 40 2 ad 1).

with other persons, as opposed to living alone, we are more like the divine persons, not less like God, and when we form communities, we go up, not down. To Personalists this rings true.

It seems to me that the basic difficulty which the Scholastics encountered when they thought about the Trinity came from their emphasis on *being*, since there is only one divine being, and from their belief that being is primarily *objective* reality as opposed to subjective experience. As I said earlier, this led them, when they asked what formally constitutes a person, to answer "individual subsistence", which in their minds was an objective reality. Personalists are not subjectivists but they give a certain priority to subjective experience and to be a person means to be (or to be capable of becoming, or to have been) a subject, so that to regard someone as a person one must know him or her as a subject and, at the risk of going too far, I will say that if a person is a subject and if we are willing to affirm a distinction between subjectivity and objective reality in God which is analogous to the distinction which we experience, we may perhaps say that at the divine level there are: one essence, nature, substance or being, three persons; one what, three whos; the divine being is ontologically one, the divine persons are psychologically three; and there are perhaps one object, three subjects.

The psychological theory

Shortly after the First Council of Constantinople, Augustine proposed what I might call a *general* theory of the Trinity, in the light of which particular ideas can be understood. He said that the two processions are analogous to our two spiritual activities, intellection and volition, or knowledge and love. The theory is now called the psychological theory. As people were looking for an understanding, in terms of an overall picture, and as this was the only one on offer, it was widely accepted. Augustine said that in an intellectual act the divine being's knowledge of the divine nature is expressed in a Word, which is distinct from its utterer, so that thanks to knowledge there are two persons. When a man has a son he communicates his own nature to his son and can see himelf in him. Similarly, the utterer of the Word communicates the divine nature to the Word and sees himself in it: so he is the Father and the Word is the Son. The love which is in the divine being is a volitional act which is the Holy Spirit, who proceeds from the first two persons.

Scholasticism: Anselm

Augustine did not go into details about the love which is involved in the second procession but later the question seems to have arisen: is it the love of the divine being for itself or the love of the first two persons for each other? Anselm said that it is the self-love of the divine being. It was maintained that nothing is willed unless it is known, which is to say that intellection precedes volition, or knowledge precedes love; therefore, it was said, there is one source of the first procession but the third person proceeds from, or is "spirated by", the first two.

It has been asked whether, according to the theologians who held this theory, the divine persons love each other *as persons*. Later exponents of the Anselmian theory replied with emphasis: "No, there is only one divine love and its object is the divine nature. The divine persons love themselves-and-each-other as the divine being, but they do not love each other as persons distinct from themselves. If they loved each other as persons there would be six loves, since each of the three would have distinct loves for the two others, but there can be only one, as there is only one one love in God". If one were to ask, "Do they even *know* one another as persons?", these authors would reply, "They know themselves-and-one-another as God".

Criticism of this theory

The principle that nothing is willed unless it is previously known is not sound, even at the human level, since in us intellection presupposes a volitional drive which is preconscious (the Scholastics called it a *voluntas ut natura* or natural as opposed to conscious will).[6] It is even more problematic to base on it an explanation of the distinction between the two processions.

Also, it seems strange to say that the divine persons are analogous to the members of a family who all love the family, and themselves and all its other members *as members of the family*, but none of whom

---

[5] See above, p. 119.
[6] Gerald O'Collins says that it is "somewhat problematic to presume *tout court* that knowing comes before willing" (*The Tripersonal God,* p. 218).

loves himself or any other as an individual person. Strange? It is downright shocking.

Moreover, in this theory, love is involved in the second procession only, which means that the first procession, in which the Father generates the Son, is utterly loveless.[7] This, too, is intolerable.

Richard of St Victor

In the twelfth century Richard of St Victor, a Scottish monk in a monastery near Paris, wrote a treatise on the Trinity which can be described as personalist, though of course the word did not then exist. He said that, since God has all perfections and charity is a perfection, there must be charity in God. But, he said, charity is love for another, for "no one is properly said to have charity for himself"; therefore in God there are at least two persons. He went on to say that from the mutual love of the first two persons a third person springs, so that there are three divine persons. Concerning the second procession proposers of the psychological theory were now divided into the Anselmians, who held that the Holy Spirit proceeds from the self-love of the divine being, and the Victorines, who held that he proceeds from the love of the first two persons for each other.[8] The Victorine or mutual-love theory had followers in the Middle Ages but in the end the Anselmian theory won general acceptance. However, in the eighteen-nineties the Victorine theory was revived by Théodore de Regnon[9] and in the years which followed it gained some support.

More recent speculation

For the most part, contemporary writers on the Trinity either hardly mention the psychological theory or they dismiss it as an aberration

---

[7] David Coffey says that according to Thomas every agent acts from love and he adds: "This must apply to the Father in the act of generating the Son" (*Deus Trinitas*, p. 49). But according to the Anselmians the only divine love is that of the divine being for itself, and they were keeping that for the second procession.

[8] See Cowburn, *Love and the Person*, pp. 258-263.

[9] De Regnon, in *Etudes de théologie positive sur le mystère de la Trinité*, wrote some marvellous passages about the love which persons have for each other as persons. He was at least a precursor of Personalism.

on which it is not worth wasting time. However, it would seem that at least some authors have proposed theories like that of Richard of St Victor. Writing in the *Revue Thomiste* in 1992, Serge-Thomas Bonino said that in *La Trinité comme histoire* (1989) Bruno Forte had used love to explain the Trinity. He went on to say that the use of love in Trinitarian theology had become common in contemporary onto-phobia but love cannot play an explanatory role in a truly scientific synthesis. Love, he said, the first act of the will, is for Thomists derived from being. It supposes a subject and a good object, i.e., being. "To think about the mystery of God, being is anterior to love and more explanatory."[10] There spoke a perfect-being theologian, a pure Scholastic. An obvious comment is that love plays an explanatory role in the Anselmian theory. More to the point, while being may in a sense be anterior to love, if someone explains the Trinity in terms of love he works at a higher level that someone who explains it in terms of being, and theologians influenced by Personalism are likely to do this, since love is a personal experience. If Bonino thinks that they have been infected by onto-phobia, they can reply that he himself suffers from onto-mania.

If Personalists choose to understand the Trinity in the light of the psychological theory, they can accept the Anselmian and Neo-Scholastic idea of the first procession, with this qualification, that it involves not only the self-knowledge but also the self-love of the divine being. They can then accept the Victorine idea of the second procession, affirming that "after" the first procession each of the first two divine persons knows and loves the other *as another person,* and that they express their love by "spirating" a third person, the Holy Spirit. In this case, the distinction between the two processions is not analogous to the distinction in us between intellection and volition or knowledge and love; it is based on the distinction between being and person—in the first procession there is the self-knowledge and self-love of the divine being *as a being,* in the second procession there is the knowledge and love of the first two persons of and for each other *as persons*—and this distinction is traditional in this context.

---

[10] Bonino, "Théologie Trinitaire", pp. 757-758.

Appropriation

Christians have traditionally assigned different actions to each of the divine persons. For instance, we say that the Father is the Creator and the Holy Spirit inspired the biblical authors and guides Church leaders now. Anselm, however, stated the principle that "everything is one in God where there is no opposition of relationship", which was taken to mean that while the three persons are distinct from one another by virtue of the relationships between them, in all their outer-directed actions they act as one being. Thomas Aquinas said: "Common to the whole divinity are all causations".[11] This means that if we say that one divine person, whom we name, does something, this is by "appropriation", which is a figure of speech, only. Concerning creation, for instance, Thomas said:

> God creates according to his existence, which is his essence, which is common to the three Persons. Hence creation is not proper to any Person but common to the whole Trinity.[12]

He also said that when in prayer we address our creator, saying "Our Father", we are actually addressing all three persons at once, not the Father as a particular person",[13] and this was quoted later by Thomists. This is why, except when they were discussing the Trinity or the Incarnation, the Scholastics were able to ignore the doctrine of the Trinity and talk all the time of God, with verbs in the singular, as if they were Unitarians.[14] I found the following in the writing of a man whom I shall not name: "In the philosophy of St Thomas, God, as infinite Esse, the pure act of existence, was a free and consciously active person". Somehow the three persons had become one.

It is one thing to say that the statement in Genesis that when God had created the world he needed a rest is metaphorical; it seems to

---

[11] *"Communia totius divinitatis sunt omnia causalia"* (Thomas, *Summa Theologica,* 1 45 6 sed contra).

[12] *"Creare convenit Deo secundum suum esse, quod est eius essentia, quae est communis tribus Personis. Unde creare non est proprium alicui Personae sed commune toti Trinitati"* (Thomas, *Summa Theologica,* 1 45 6 c). Only the second divine person became man but this, according to the Scholastics, was not an action, properly speaking.

[13] *"Cum Deo dicimus, Pater noster, hoc pertinet ad totam Trinitatem"* (Thomas, *Summa Theologica,* 3 23 2 sed contra).

[14] See above, p. 135-136.

me another to say that all talk of any divine person doing this or that in the world is basically metaphorical. Also, the Anselmian principle implies that the doctrine of the Trinity is irrelevant to us as we live our lives, since always we are dealing with the one God, as one, and this to to put too wide a gulf between theology and life. The Trinity should be a real mystery of life for us and we should be communicating not so much with the one divine nature as with the three divine persons. The Sabellian heresy, which I mentioned earlier, was a denial of the *immanent Trinity*, the doctrine of appropriation implies that there is no such thing as an *economic Trinity*, and there are both.

Chapter 12

God to Us: The Scholastic Theory and Criticism of It

The enormous amount of multiplicity in creatures created a problem for the Scholastics, who loved unity and associated it with truth and goodness. The problem was: How can God be involved with creatures without losing some of his unity and hence some of his goodness? They solved this problem to some extent by unifying the divine knowledge and action so far as was possible. I shall summarise their view of God's actions in the created universe, his knowledge of it and his attitude towards it; I shall then offer some criticism of this view and make suggestions for a Personalist approach to the question.

THE SCHOLASTIC THEORY

Some metaphysical ideas

The idea of God as "prime mover"
Aristotle said that the divine being is the "prime mover" which was taken by Christians to imply that God is the absolutely first cause of all things and events. At times a person in a high position tells a second person to deal with a certain problem, the second person tells a third person to write a letter, and he or she does so and gives it to a fourth person to polish and type; in which case we might say that the action came from the first person in that series. That is not what Aristotle meant by prime mover. In the divine case the prime mover, the divine being, is actively causing secondary causes to act *as they act*.

That God has total control of events
Augustine strongly affirmed God's control and from him came the idea of a "Christian philosophy of history", according to which God

is at work in all that happens. Thomas maintained that God's will is always done[1] and the Neo-Scholastics affirmed this. For instance, in *Foundations of Thomistic Philosophy*, published in French in 1927, Antonin-Gilbert Sertillanges said:

> In order to have a right idea of Providence, we must know whether God's will is always obeyed. We give an affirmative answer to this question, because God is the universal cause of universal being, and all being must obey his law. A cause infallibly attains its effect unless impeded by something which is not subject to it. Since God is the cause of all things, nothing can escape his causality and therefore nothing can impede the complete realisation of his effects.[2]

If, aiming at a target, I fire an arrow into the air and a gust of wind carries it off course so that I miss, this is because while I can aim an arrow I cannot control the air. But God controls everything, therefore "his action always attains its end. Everything he created is according to his pre-established plan."[3]

That God wills the whole

I said earlier that according to at least some Scholastics value is situated in the whole universe rather than in any element or elements of it.[4] This implies that God wills the universe, in both its spatial and temporal dimensions, as a whole; he wills particular beings in it only as elements of it. In a good production of a play, the actions of many people are praised and rewarded *according to the contribution which they make to the play as a whole.* If the actors and others working on the play benefit by it, so much the better, but that is not the purpose of the performance. If the director takes a particular actor aside and works with him on a scene, this might help the actor in his career, but that would not be why the director takes him aside. There are these differences between God and that theatre director: the production of a play is not anyone's whole life, whereas God's action is directed at everyone in his or her entirety; it takes some weeks or months to produce a play, whereas in creation whole lives are involved, from

---

[1] *"Necesse est voluntatem Dei semper impleri"* (Thomas, *Summa Theologica*, 1 19 6 c).
[2] Sertillanges, *Foundations of Thomistic Philosophy*, p. 141.
[3] Ibid. p. 148.
[4] See above, p. 114.

Chapter 12: *God to Us: The Scholastic Theory & Criticism of It*   157

birth to death; finally, the play is in the end a fiction whereas creation involves real persons.

Thomas put the scholastic position clearly. In the *Summa Contra Gentiles* he said:

> A particular good is ordered to the good of the universe as a means to an end, or as imperfect thing to a perfect thing.... It follows that the good of the universe is the reason why God wills every particular good in the universe."[5]

He went on:"God wills the existence of human beings so that the universe will be complete",[6] and he said: "What is most good in created things is the good of the whole universe" and "therefore the good of the whole order of created things is what God primarily wills and intends". In the *Summa Theologica* he said: "What is best in things is the good of the order of the universe" and "The good of the universe is therefore what God properly intends".[7]

He said that God first decided how big the universe would be and so determined the number of creatures.[8] That is, he said that God is not like a man who, wanting to build a house, sees how many bricks he has and lets that determine how big the house will be; he is like a man who decides how big his house will be and lets that determine how many bricks he obtains. He also said that God created in order to communicate his goodness and that while some beings represent some aspects of this and other beings represent other aspects, the universe as a whole comes nearer to representing it than any particular creature can come: that is, God's creative purpose is best achieved in the universe as a whole, and that is what he primarily wills. Thomas was not here talking about things as distinct from persons. "Among all creatures,"he said, "rational creatures are most principally ordered to the good of the universe."[9]

[5] *"Bonum particulare ordinatur ad bonum totius sicut ad finem, ut imperfectum ad perfectum.... Relinquitur ergo quod bonum universi sit ratio quare Deus vult unumquodque particulare bonum in universo."* (Thomas, Summa Contra Gentiles, I,86.)

[6] *"Deus vult hominem esse ad hoc quod completio universi sit"* (ibid.).

[7] *"Ordo igitur universi est proprie a Deo intentus"* (Thomas, Summa Theologica, 1 15 2 c).

[8] *"Praeordinavit in qua mensura deberet esse totum universum"* (ibid., 1 23 7 c).

[9] Quoted above, p. 116.

The one divine decision

God, the Scholastics said, does not make trillions of creative decisions, one for every creature and every event in the universe, but "pictures" the whole universe and everything that happens in it in one simple "look", in one single decision says "Let it be", and it is. He is like a theatre director who says, "We'll do *Hamlet* next", and from that one decision comes eventually the performance of the play, which has many words and actions.

By fairly general agreement in the Catholic Church, there are two "orders" or ensembles of reality. They used to be called the natural and supernatural orders, or the orders of nature and grace, and they came from two decrees or decisions, those of creation and elevation. It was generally believed by Catholics that when God created human beings with bodies like ours he had to provide air, water, food and so on, so that human beings and what is necessary for them to lead human lives were contained in a single decision, that of "creation". The divine persons did not, however, have to offer human beings a share in their personal life. Nevertheless, they did this and it is a gift or grace as the necessities of life are not. It is the matter of a distinct decision, that of "elevation". One can picture a married couple deciding to have a child; in making this decision they implicitly commit themselves to feeding the child when it comes and giving it everything to which it will have a right. They might at the same time decide to send the child to a private school, though he or she will not have a right to this and this decision is not implicit in their decision to have a child. In this case we can see two decisions, distinct from one another, which are made at the same time. In a similar way, according to the scholastics, "creation" and "elevation" involve two decrees which are made together.

The scholastics generally said that God is "outside time" and that he is not comparable to a human father who, when his children grow up, makes decision after decision about them as circumstances change. He is more like the theatre director who decides to put on *Hamlet*, so that of any event we are able to say: "Before time began, God decided that this would happen at this time".

The problem of non-moral "evil"

This was the foundation of a certain Christian optimism, which has often been expressed. For instance, in a book which was published in 1609 and which thousands of religious (including me) had to read, Alphonsus Rodriguez said that whatever happens is the will of God, who "lets nothing pass [happen] but what contributes, in a special manner, to our greater good and profit"; he said that "all that comes from him"—and that means everything—"will turn to our profit and advantage".[10] In the eighteenth century Alexander Pope expressed the idea in verse:

> *All nature is but art, unknown to thee;*
> *All chance, direction, which thou canst not see;*
> *All discord, harmony not understood;*
> *All partial evil, universal good;*
> *And, spite of pride, in erring reason's spite,*
> *One truth is clear: Whatever is, is right".*[11]

The divine non-passivity

That God is pure act

Aristotle and the scholastics said that, being pure act, the divine being is in no way passive and hence is not at all receptive of causal influence. George A. Blair writes: "If activity becomes more immanent the higher one goes in the scale of being, it is more reasonable to assume (as both Aristotle and St Thomas did) that the highest is totally immanent".[12] This means that there is nothing in God, including knowledge, which has a source outside him.

The divine knowledge of creatures

We have two kinds of knowledge. If I go to see a new building, I walk round outside it and in it and after some hours I may feel that I know it, so that I can describe it to people. This is spectator-knowledge, which is true or false depending on whether or not it corresponds to the building, which, one may say, exists in reality *and then* in my head. On the other hand, if an architect designs a building and he is sure

---

[10] Rodriguez, "Treatise on Conformity to the Will of God", chap. 10.
[11] Pope, *An Essay on Man*, I, lines 285-294.
[12] Blair, "On Esse and Relation", p. 162.

that it will be or later was built according to his plans, it exists in his head *and then* in reality; he has the idea of it or he "knows" it before it is built and when it has been built he does not need to look at it in order to form an idea of it. According to the Scholastics, God has no spectator-knowledge or knowledge which conforms to things which exist prior to his knowledge of them. *All* his knowledge of creatures is analogous to that of the architect. Peter Geach, an English philosopher, expresses a Thomist view when he says:

> God's knowledge of the world is to be compared not to our speculative [spectator] knowledge but to our knowledge of our own deeds before we do them; and all Truth is in him, in that his idea, like an artist's designs, are the measure and cause of what happens in the world: not because his thoughts reflect what happens.[13]

One can imagine a new play being performed before an audience, who sit through it wondering whether the couple in it are going to get married at the end of the play or not. They have no influence on this and are purely passive as they wait to see what happens. For the author of the play things are different: he does not need to attend a performance in order to learn what happens at the end: *he* decided whether the couple get married or not *and so* he knows. God, for the scholastics, is analogous to the author, not the audience, with this difference: the author can, if he chooses, attend a performance and just watch the play as it unfolds, but God cannot watch what happens in the universe. In Blair's terms, he is "wholly immanent" and knows things *only* in being conscious of his own thoughts and decisions.

The divine purpose

Since, according to the Scholastics, the end or purpose of a being or an action is one of its causes, called "the final cause",[14] the other Scholastic belief that no creature can have a causal influence on God implies that no creature can be or contain the purpose of a divine action, or that no creature can move God to do anything. His motive for acting must always be within himself. An accepted idea was that the final cause of divine actions is *the divine nature as communicable*. Thomas says: "God's love for his own goodness is the cause of the

---

[13] Geach, *Providence and Evil*, p. 81.
[14] See above, p. 87-88.

creation of things".[15] If someone were to tell you a truth not because he thought that it would be good for you to know it but because he loved the truth and for this reason wanted it to be more widely known, you would benefit from his action but your benefit would not be precisely what he intended; according to the view I am expounding, analogously to this God's actions benefit us but this is not precisely his intention. He is moved not by a desire to do us good but by love of his own nature, which he wants to communicate.

This implies that our own aim in life should not be our own good, the good of any human being or persons, or the success of any human cause: we were made by God for his sake and should aim at realising this aim. It also implies that a superior can say of subjects: "God does not love these persons for their own sakes, and neither do I: they have been created for his sake and if I want them to glorify God by doing things which will make their lives miserable, I shall have no qualms about telling them to do them".

The divine impassibility

Aristotle maintained that the eternal substance has no passions or feelings; he said that God is "impassible".[16] This was re-affirmed by Philo (ca. 20 BC–AD 40), an Alexandrian Jew who wrote *On the Unchangeableness of God*,[17] in which he interpreted the scriptures in a way that was influenced by Greek philosophers. He reinforced Aristotle's influence and it came to be generally believed by Christians that God is impassible. In the third century a profession of faith began:

---

[15] *"Amor igitur quo suam bonititatem amat est causa creationis rerum"* (Thomas, *Summa Contra Gentiles*, 4 20).

[16] The word translated as "impassible" is, in Greek, the adjective which corresponds to the noun *apatheia*. Some Greek words were taken into Latin with slightly changed spelling, and with another change in spelling they passed into English (this is the case with "eucharist"). If this had happened with the word used by Aristotle in this context, we would be saying that God is apathetic. Other Greek words were translated with existing Latin words, which later came into English. Fortunately, this happened here: *apatheia* became *impassibilitas* and then "impassibility".

[17] Weinandy devotes eight pages to Philo in *Does God Suffer?* "Unchangeable" is *atrepton*, a word which Aristotle had used for past events (*De mundo*, # 7,410 b 20).

"I believe in God the Father, omnipotent, invisible and impassible"[18] and in the Middle Ages Aristotelian scholastics deduced this, as another aspect of God's non-receptivity, from the belief that he is pure act. Maritain said that we speak metaphorically when we say that creatures please God or give him joy.[19] This was taken to mean that God does not suffer when others suffer, which is to say that God the Father did not sympathise with his suffering Son and that no divine person sympathises with suffering creatures: Thomas said that it is not possible for God to be sad because of the suffering of another.[20] At the time of the Reformation, this was not an issue, so that, in the centuries which followed, theologians of all churches believed in the divine impassibility, which is affirmed in the first of the Thirty-Nine Articles of the Church of England.

Another argument was used. If *per impossibile* there was an infinitely rich man, it would be impossible by giving him a finite amount of money to make him richer or by taking a finite amount of money from him to make him less rich, because infinity plus or minus a finite amount equals infinity, as before. God is infinitely happy and so, as Maritain said, nothing can be added to or taken away from the divine beatitude.[21] That is, he is not emotionally affected, one way or the other, by what we do.

Understandably, there were some dissident voices. In the fourth century Lactantius said: "What beatitude could there be in God, if he was always quiet and unmoveable *(immobilis),* if he was deaf to our prayers and blind to those who worship him?"[22] Thomas B. Weinandy says of Lactantius that "because his treatise is primarily pastoral rather than philosophical ... he does not significantly advance the discussion",[23] that is, it is lowbrow theology, like the many sermons in which preachers attribute human emotions to God.

[18] This is from a commentary, written around the year 404, on a profession of faith in Aquileia, which was an important city at the north end of the Adriatic. Denziger-Schönmetzer, *Enchiridion,* # 16.
[19] Maritain, "Quelques réflexions", p. 19.
[19] *"Tristari ergo de miseria alterius non competit Deo"* (Thomas, *Summa Theologica,* 1 21 3 c).
[21] Maritain, "Quelques réflexions", p. 19.
[22] Lactantius, *De ira Dei,* chap. 4.
[23] Weinandy, *Does God Suffer?,* p. 106.

God's love of creatures

The Scholastics who said that God *wills* the whole universe and particular beings only as elements of it also said that God *loves* the universe, and human beings only as elements of it, like someone enjoying the notes of a melody only as elements of it.[24] Those who said that likeness or unity is the principle of love said that God loves us for what we have in common with him, and, because every perfection which we have is from him, we have more in common with him that with any other being and that therefore he loves us more than anyone else loves us.

The view that the only possible direct object of the divine will is the divine goodness implies that God loves creatures only indirectly, as participations of his goodness. What this means can be explained by means of an analogy, which I shall set as if it were a quotation:

> A great composer-pianist believes that he plays his own works perfectly and he listens with complete satisfaction to recordings of himself playing them. He takes pupils and sets out to teach them how to play his works "as they should be played", by which he means as he himself plays them. Some pupils come close to that, so that few people can detect any difference between tape-recordings which the pupils make and recordings which the composer himself has made. The composer enjoys listening to these pupils playing. His enjoyment is somewhat diminished by the few passages in which they do not exactly reproduce his performances, so that listening to them is never as good as listening to recordings of himself, but he does not let these passages spoil his pleasure. When a pupil finishes playing a work, then, the great man says: "Well done, I enjoyed that". On the one hand, the pupil likes being praised, but on the other hand he says later to his friends: "The maestro did not enjoy listening to *me*. He only enjoyed listening to his own performance reproduced by me. Where his own compositions are concerned, he is completely self-centred. I have worked with other composer-pianists and at times, after I have played one of their pieces, they have said that while I did not play it as they themselves play it, they enjoyed my interpretation of it and will listen to it again. They were able to appreciate *me*, as this man is not."

---

[24] See above, p. 122.

According to classical Scholastic thought, God is like the self-centred composer-pianist in this story.

People who have many good qualities are more similar to God, or have more in common with him, than people who lack them. The Scholastic theory therefore implies that God loves great people more than others. Sertillanges said: "God must have love—not passionate or emotional but intellectual love.... . He loves all things, since all participate in the Sovereign Good.... . But it follows that he loves them unequally."[25] God, he said, wills the differences which exist between human beings, and "these differences allow the creative love to be qualified and graduated". Thomas even went so far as to say that, other things being equal, God loves kings more than ordinary people because he and they have more in common.[26]

The indwelling

It is Christian teaching that the Holy Spirit dwells in "the souls of the just". This is explained by Scholastic thinkers in terms of being: a being is where it acts, they say, and in so far as God is the cause of all things he is in all things, and in so far as he causes sanctifying grace to exist in our souls he is in our souls in a particular way, which we call the indwelling and which we appropriate to the Holy Spirit. The indwelling is then ontologically or objectively real and while we may know about it and be grateful for it, it is not in essence an element of our experience.

CRITICISM OF THIS PERFECT-BEING THEOLOGY

Christianity includes a world-picture or "theory" which Christians are expected to have in their minds and to some extent understand, and

---

[25] Sertillanges, *The Foundations of Scholastic Philosophy*, p. 143.
[26] "A king is especially similar to God since he does in his kingdom what God does in the world *(dum agit in regno quod Deus in mundo)*.... . But a being is more acceptable to God the more it resembles him *(tanto est aliquid Deo acceptius quanto magis ad eius imitationem accedit)*.... . The consequence of this is that good kings are most acceptable to God and will be most highly rewarded by him *(consequens igitur est bonos reges Deo esse acceptissimos et ab eo maxime praemiandos)*." (Thomas, *On Kingship*, chap. 9, # 72; see bibliography.)

Scholastic Theology is the result of striving to achieve this. But in the first place Christianity is a message to be taken to heart and *lived,* and the Church also needs reflection on the subjective, personal experience of being a Christian, and this is where Personalism comes in.

I shall not waste time dismissing the idea that value resides in wholes of which persons are members, the idea that outside God the ultimate all-inclusive whole is the created universe, and the idea that God wills this, and human beings only as elements of it.

If God in his activity has no "end" other than himself, there is no altruism in God, and if he is "totally immanent" he is utterly self-centred. But we say in our profession of faith that the Son of God became man "for us men and for salvation" and "for our sake he was crucified". I for one refuse to believe that these are superficial pious utterances which do not express the deep reality. I gave an analogy earlier of a great pianist who appreciates the playing of his students only in so far as they reproduce his works as he himself plays them. One of them says, "He does not appreciate me, only himself", and it is shocking to think of God being like this.

Also, it may be humiliating to be forced to do something which we do not want to do, either because someone is making us do it or because we need the money, but to do something for another person whom one loves, and to do it of one's own accord, is not at all humiliating and entails no submission to another or to the pressure of circumstances. It is not, therefore, wrong to say that a divine action has a "final cause" which is a human person.

The idea of control

I said earlier that the idea that God has total control over all events, so that he decides everything we do, is incompatible with belief in human free will and responsibility. Also, we do not now believe that parents should attempt totally to control the adult lives of their sons and daughters. On the contrary, they should allow their sons and daughters to choose for themselves their life's works and their spouses. They should do this not because they lack knowledge but because as persons the sons and daughters have a right to respect. Similarly, we should attribute to God a respect for human beings as persons.

According to the Scholastics, if some men are playing poker, God has from all eternity decided that they will play, what hands each of them will be dealt, what bets they will make and how much they will win or lose. I find it hard to believe that anyone plays poker believing that. It seems to me, for one, to be more reasonable to suppose that God lets nature, which in a poker game includes chance, take its course.

The divine knowledge

When total control is denied, the Scholastic theory of divine knowledge goes with it, since according to that theory God knows human actions only by virtue of the fact that he decides them. Norris Clarke says: "It seems to me that we must resolutely affirm that God's knowledge of our free actions in determined by us in some significant sense".[27] This, which implies a rejection of total control, is surely true.

It also implies that if we do not *actually* make decisions, God does not have knowledge of them, because there is nothing to know. If (as did not happen) I had found myself last night having to choose between working on this book or watching *Persona,* God does not know what I would have done. To say this is not to attribute ignorance to God, since ignorance is not knowing something which has a definite reality of some kind: it is like saying that God does not know the last digit of the square root of two when it is expressed as a decimal (for the benefit of non-mathematicians let me explain that there is no last digit: they go on for ever). Also, God does not know whether, if I were to be asked tomorrow to give a certain lecture, I would say yes or no. That is, what I have said amounts to another denial of Molinism.

With this, too, goes the idea of God being "outside time" because by one decision, prior to all events, he decides all that happens in the universe. God must know decisions as they are made, which is in time. John Paul II has said: "God's revelation is therefore immersed in time and history" and "History therefore becomes for humanity the arena where we see what God does for humanity".[28]

---

[27] Clarke, *Explorations in Metaphysics,* p. 305. This is from a 1973 article.
[28] John Paul II, *Fides et Ratio,* ## 11,12.

The divine non-sympathy

In the nineteenth century, the doctrine of impassibility, which had been affirmed by theologians of all churches for centuries, began to be denied.[29] In Germany, in the eighteen-fifties, Isaak August Dormer wrote *Divine Immutability: A Critical Reconsideration* and in England in 1893 A. M. Fairbairn said: "Theology has no falser idea than the impassibility of God".[30] In 1928 B. R. Brasnett said: "Men feel, and perhaps will feel increasingly, that a God who is not passible, who is exempt from pain and suffering, is a God of little value to suffering humanity".[31] In 1974 Jürgen Moltmann said: "Were God incapable of suffering in any respect, … he would also be incapable of love".[32] Writing in France in 1975, François Varillon said that he was afraid that "the image of an impassible God, looking down, with olympic serenity, on the evil and misery of the world remains and pursues its secret existence in the depths of mankind's unconscious",[33] though I doubt whether its existence was secret. In 1988 P. Fiddes said: "If God is not less than personal, and if the claim that 'God is love' is to have any recognisable continuity with our normal experience of love, the conclusion seems inescapable that a loving God must be a sympathetic and therefore a suffering God".[34] In 1994 a group of Protestant theologians in Canada and the United States produced *The Openness of God: A Biblical Challenge to the Traditional Understanding of God*, which is an eloquent attack on impassibility. Thomas G. Weinandy said in 2000 that he had been teaching theology since 1975 and had been aware during that time that the majority of theologians (I presume he meant both Catholics and Protestants) believed in a suffering God, and in a huge number of books and articles had argued for this belief, which he himself did not share.[35] Consider this story:

---

[29] In *Does God Suffer?*, chap. 1, pp. 1-16, Weinandy gives a long and detailed account of the authors who have attacked impassibility. Most of the quotations which I shall give have come from there.
[30] Fairbairn, *The Place of Christ in Modern Theology*, p. 483.
[31] Brasnett, *The Suffering of the Impassible God*, p. ix.
[32] Moltmann, *The Crucified God*, p. 230.
[33] Varillon, *The Humility and Suffering of God*, p. 129.
[34] Fiddes, *The Creative Suffering of God*, p. 17.
[35] Weinandy, *Does God Suffer?*, p. vii.

There was a family consisting of a mother, father and several children. One evening word came that one of the sons had been hit by a car, badly hurt and taken to hospital, where he was being operated on. In great distress, the mother and father rushed to the hospital, where they were told that their son's life was in danger. For some hours they suffered and then at last they were told that he would live and he was wheeled out of the theatre. On the one hand, as they looked at their battered son they felt great sorrow; on the other hand, they were overwhelmed with joy at the thought that he was going to live and be all right.

In this story, the parents were not themselves wounded and they did not become less intelligent or virtuous than they had been; but they experienced both sorrow and joy because of what happened to their son. In an analogous way, when human beings suffer or succeed, objectively the divine being does not become less perfect in any way but subjectively the divine persons experience sorrow or joy. Sympathy is a virtuous act of which they are capable.

The indwelling

In the fifth century the pseudo-Denis said, "Love is ecstatic" and Thomas, who believed that the words had been written by the real Denis, often quoted this. On his own account he said:

> The lover is in the beloved in as much as he regards the goods and bads of the beloved as his own, and the will of the beloved as his own, so that as it were in his beloved he is affected by the good and ill that befall the beloved.[36]

Here he says that the lover is subjectively in the beloved's subjectivity, and this is how the indwelling should be explained. It is not a matter of physical, ontological causation: it is psychological or subjective.

---

[36] Thomas, *Summa Theologica*, 1-2 28 2 c.

Chapter 13

Human Beings to God in Scholastic and Personalist Theology

Faith

Two conceptions of faith

Let me give two cases:

(1) While a couple were out for an evening, a burglar broke a window of their house, let himself in and stole some goods. They reported this to the police and a detective asked a next-door neighbour if he had heard anything. The neighbour replied that at 10 p.m. he had heard a sound of breaking glass. He knew the exact time, he said, because it was just at the end of the film *Titanic,* which he had been watching on television. He had gone round his house, checked the windows, found nothing broken and gone back to watch the news. The detective thanked him, checked the television guide, made sure of when *Titanic* had ended and in his mind fixed the time of the break-in at 10 p.m. Subsequently he interviewed a man whom he had reason to suspect and asked him where he had been on the night in question. The man said that between seven and ten-thirty he had been having dinner with a friend at a certain restaurant. The waiter, he said, would confirm this. The detective later spoke to the waiter, who said that the man had been there; not only that, when he was serving coffee the man had asked him what time it was and he had replied "Ten o'clock"; the pair left about half an hour later. "That settles it," said the detective to himself, "it wasn't him".

(2) A single man and a single woman had been meeting often and getting to know one another. One day the woman said: "Starting when I was ten, in Norway, my father made me pose for nude photographs once a month. He insisted that the purpose was proper and he showed the photos to all the members, mostly men, of a photography club to which he belonged. He intended to continue

until I was eighteen, then publish a selection of the photos showing the development of my body from ten to eighteen. I hated it but my mother, though she did not like it, told me to do as I was told and I obeyed. My father died when I was sixteen, my mother and I destroyed all the photos and two years later I emigrated, leaving her. I am now pathologically modest—for instance, I never go swimming or even play tennis—and I attribute this to what I see was a form of sexual abuse." Moved, the man thanked the woman. He had been thinking of asking her to marry him and what she had said did not make him drop the idea.

There is a certain similarity between these two stories, since in each of them a man believes, on another person's word, something which he has not himself observed. There are, however, great differences between the two beliefs.

(1) In the first situation, the detective might wish that he had himself been outside the house on the night in question and had seen with his own eyes who broke into the house; the neighbour is a sort of second best. This is not the case in the second story.

(2) In the first situation, what is important to the detective is the information; the neighbour is merely its source. In the second situation, what is of primary importance is the speaker. The man's attention is fixed on the woman, and he is interested in her story because of what it means that she tells it to him.

(3 In the first situation, there is no personal relationship between the neighbour and the detective. In the second situation, as John Paul II says, the man's belief in what the woman tells him is "humanly richer than mere evidence, because it involves an interpersonal relationship",[1] which it takes to a new level.

(4) The difference between the two assents becomes apparent if we imagine what would happen in both cases if the listener were to find out that what he had been told was not true. If in the first case the detective were later to learn that the screening of *Titanic* had been cancelled at the last minute and another film had been substituted, he would at once conclude that the man in the restaurant was probably the burglar, with the neighbour acting as his accomplice. He would say to himself, "That settles that". In the second case, if the man were to learn that the woman's father had died when she was nine, he would

---

[1] John Paul II, *Fides et Ratio*, # 32.

say to himself that the woman was either a liar or psychotic, he would drop the idea of proposing marriage, and he would feel as if his whole future was like a house that had come crashing down.

According to Scholastic theologians, a human being learns that God has revealed certain things, judges that God always tells the truth and, on God's word, believes them. When the act of faith is understood in this way, it is analogous to the detective's assent to what the neighbour says, with this difference, that whereas the neighbour might be mistaken or lying, God is entirely reliable. The primary object of faith is a truth, which is something which we do not ourselves observe. In Personalist theology, the act of faith is a human being's free decision to listen to the divine persons, to believe them and so to enter into personal relationships with them. When Wojtyla studied in Rome in 1946-48, he wrote his thesis on John of the Cross and the act of faith, and he is said to have "emphasised the personal nature of the human encounter with God".[2] In the following year, 1949, Jean Mouroux's book, *Je crois en toi,* was published: the title meant that the act of faith is expressed not in the words, "I believe what God has revealed" but in the words, "I believe you", addressed to the divine persons.[3] John Paul II says that when people have faith, their assent to truth is "set within the context of interpersonal communication",[4] that is, it is analogous to the man believing the woman in the case I gave above, not to the detective believing what he was told by the neighbour.

This means that having the Christian faith is not, in the first place, believing everything in Thomas's *Summa,* Calvin's *Institutes, The Catholic Catechism* or any other statement of Christian beliefs. It is having personal relationships with the divine persons. This means that if someone is convinced by "natural reason" that God exists, his final state is not Christian faith; indeed, if he were to study various religions and, as an outside observer, judge that what Christians believe is most probably true, this would not be Christian faith. In Buber's language, Christian faith is an I-Thou experience.

[2] See above, p. 73-74.
[3] The full title of Mouroux's book is *Je crois en toi: Structure personnelle de la foi,* which means *I Believe in You: The Personal Structure of Faith.* The English translation is *I Believe.* Whoever gave it that title either had not read the book or had not understood it.
[4] John Paul II, *Fides et Ratio,* # 13.

In ordinary conversation we would be more likely to say that the detective believed the neighbour than that he had faith in him, and if we say that we have faith in someone we do not mean, primarily, that we believe what he or she says. Often the word "faith" in translations of the scriptures corresponds to our word "confidence", which I presume is derived ultimately from *fides,* which means "faith", and its primary object is a person rather than something which someone has said. For instance, if a woman who is about to be married says that while her parents are distrustful of her fiancé she herself has faith in him, she does not mean, at least not primarily, that she believes that things which he has told her are, as a matter of fact, true. She means that she is sure that their relationship is on a sound basis and that she has the confidence which a person getting married needs. Thus the Personalist understanding of Christian faith corresponds better than the Scholastic understanding to our ordinary understanding of the word "faith".

This is not to say that Christian faith has nothing to do with any beliefs *about* God. On the contrary, every *Thou* is also a *He* or a *She,* it is impossible to know someone personally without knowing something *about* him or her, hence a "belief in" God which included no "beliefs that" would not make sense. So Christian faith presupposes the assent to the truth that God exists and speaks to us in Christ and it leads us to assent to many truths which God has revealed to us.

The freedom and certainty of the act of faith
The Scholastics believed the Catholic teaching that the act of faith is free, which seemed to mean that the evidence for it did not compel assent. They also had to believe that faith is the strongest of all certainties. This gave them the problem of explaining how it can be rational to assent to something as certain when the evidence for it is not compelling. Also, if faith is understood as believing certain truths, it is not easy to see how we can be more sure of the truths of the Christian faith than, for instance, of our own existence.

In a Personalist understanding of faith, the "certainty" or firmness of the act of faith is the strength of the commitment to the divine persons which someone makes when he or she enters into relationships with them, and this commitment is both firm and free. A Personalist theory of faith turns out to be intellectually satisfying in ways that Scholastic theories were not.

The approach to faith

Scholastics insisted that the approach of an adult to the Christian faith must be based on objective factors: if one is dealing with an inquiring adult, one should prove the existence of God using Thomas's Five Ways, then the accuracy of the gospels and the truth of their stories about miracles, and one should deduce from them that Christ must be a divine being. Some contemporary theologians go to the opposite extreme and concede no place to reasoning in the approach of an adult to the Christian fath, but this not true of all Personalists. One can regard reasoning as important, even in most cases necessary, while believing that when people make the final step they are not like a juror who, hearing a decisive piece of evidence, says to himself or herself, "That settles it"; they are like someone who agrees to engage in personal conversation with another person and to believe what he or she says, so establishing a personal relationship.

Hope and charity: our love of God

Scholastic philosophers maintained that the object of the will is the good. They also maintained that being, only being, is good. It followed that the acts of our wills can be directed only to beings. As God is one being, this means that we hope in and love the one divine being, as the omnipotent and infinitely perfect being. Also, because of their intellectualism Scholastic philosophers tended to stress, and to spend most time studying, *knowledge* of the real and to avoid the topic of love.[5] Similarly, Scholastic theologians seem to have believed that of faith, hope and charity the greatest is faith, because it is intellectual and fundamental, though of course they did not expressly say this.

Personalist theologians do not deny that we appreciate the infinite perfection of the divine nature but above this they put a love which, like friendship and married love, is love of persons as such. We have three loves rather than one, since there are three persons, and we express our love in communication or prayer, in attention, in loyalty,

---

[5] See above, p. 121.

in respect for other persons whom the divine persons also love, and perhaps in the enjoyment of life.

Also, if two persons love one another as persons, each gives himself or herself to the other and each accepts or receives the other. Each is profoundly grateful to the other for the gift which the other has made, and rejoices in it, but it is wrong to analyse this in terms of being or in terms of potency and act. If you are talking about non-personal transactions, it may be true that beings can receive only in so far as they have lacks, but if this principle were to be applied to personal love it would mean that all love is between a have who loves and a have-not who is loved, whereas personal love at its highest is between two haves, who both give and both receive. Let me tell another story.

> One of the world's richest men is a widower who has far more money than he needs. Therefore, if you want him to do something which he does not want to do, there is no point in offering him money, and if you want something which he has and with which he does not want to part, it is a waste of time to offer him money for it. He has met a widow and he and she are attracted to one another. They both think that they will probably get married and they hope that this will happen, but they do not want to rush things and at present they are spending time together hoping, as they tell their friends, that "something will come of it". The woman has a daughter aged three who one day tells the man that she has a present for him. "What is it?", he asks, and she produces a shiny dollar coin, which she solemnly gives to him. The woman is amused as the idea of anyone giving a dollar to an immensely rich man, but the man is not at all amused. Instead, he is deeply moved, accepts the gift, thanks the little girl and tells her that he will treasure it. He has seen that the gift conveyed a message, which was: "I hope that you and my mother will get married and that you will become my stepfather". The little girl has shown that it is possible to give a big present to the richest man in the world.

The Scholastics seem to me to say that because God lacks nothing it is impossible to give him anything, but the divine persons do not have us as persons unless we give ourselves to them, as by loving them we do, and our love gives them joy.[6]

---

[6] See above, p. 161-162, where I discuss the idea that God is impassible.

According to the Scholastics, God is loved for the infinite perfections which reason leads us to attribute to him. History does not come into it.[7] According to personalists, persons reveal themselves as persons in their words and actions, which are historical, and we love Jesus, the person, who is revealed to us in his words and actions, told in the gospels.

Grace and the sacraments

For a long time, Scholastic theologians defined sanctifying grace as a fluid entity which inheres in the soul whether the person is conscious of it or not; or they said that it is "created actuation by uncreated act",[8] which again is an objective reality. They went on to say that it is supernatural as distinct fom natural.

The Scholastics understood the sacraments in ontological terms. Their primary model of a sacrament was infant baptism, in which there is no subjective experience of a religious kind and in which, when the action is correctly performed, by virtue of a contractual obligation God puts into the infant's soul the ontological entity which is sanctifying grace. There was also no subjective religious experience when an unconscious dying person was given what was then called extreme unction. In these cases the grace of the sacrament was conferred *ex opere operato,* or from the work done. It was said that in other sacraments a proper subjective disposition was required, but this was minimal in children receiving their first communion and all that was required later was that the person not have an evil attitude when receiving the sacrament, so that if young people went to communion or got married in church in order to please their parents, this was sufficient because this is not an evil intention. Quite recently I had a conversation with an elderly priest who was worried because many young Catholic adults have not received the sacrament of confirmation; he was worried not about what this implies about their subjective attitude towards the Church, but because in their childhood they had missed out on "the grace of the sacrament" which they should have received *ex opere operato.* In

[7] See above, p. 98-99, where I talk about the scholastics' lack of a sense of history.
[8] This is an example of the way in which Neo-Scholastics used technical language which was unintelligible to most people. See above, p. 97.

all this, subjective experience is considered to be sometimes necessary but never essential.

In Personalist theology, sanctifying grace is understood in personal or I-Thou terms, and to be in a state of grace means in the first place to have, as a subject, positive relationships with the divine persons. In reception of the sacraments, in so far as this involves these relationships, we encounter the divine persons and the experience of this matters. This is most obvious when the eucharist is being studied. When he dealt with this subject, a Scholastic theologian in imagination looked at a consecrated host and asked, "How can that, as a matter of objective fact, be the body of Christ?" He found his answer in transubstantiation, which supposes a theory of substance and accident, and quantity and qualities, which do not enter into the experience of receiving communion. He did not in imagination put himself into the subjectivity of someone receiving communion and ask: "What does it mean, in personal terms, to eat the body of Christ?" He left that to experts in spirituality, whose business was subjective experience. Jesus, however, changed bread and wine into his body and blood precisely in order to give them to us to eat and drink; he did not say only, "This is my body"; he said, "Take this and eat, this my body". To understand this sacrament, then, we should reflect on eating and drinking as experiences, and especially on what is experienced when one person gives food and drink to another, whom he or she loves. The objective question is important, but secondary.

Prayer

That God is impassible meant to scholastics that our prayers may produce effects in us but do not move or affect God in any way. George A. Blair writes: "God 'hears' my prayers in being the primary (though not determining) cause of the (finite) activities which are my prayers, not by being affected by them, or even being 'receptive' to them".[9] This is bad prose and worse theology.

For a long time, Catholic liturgy was thought of as an activity which gives glory to God when it is done well, more or less as the Trooping of the Colour gives glory to the monarch when the soldiers are in clean,

---

[9] Blair, "On Esse and Relation", p. 164.

neat uniforms, when their equipment is polished, and when masses of men move in absolutely exact order. For the organisers of the Trooping of the Colour, what matters is not whether the soldiers enjoy or even understand what they do: what matters is that the show go on and that everything be done strictly according to the rules; and the masters of ceremonies at Catholic liturgies had a similar attitude. Then men appeared who saw liturgical services as activities in which, ideally, the persons who form a community express their faith and their feelings. This led them to promote measures to enable everyone present at a liturgy to understand what is going on and to participate actively in it. In this way the changes in the Catholic liturgy correspond to the switch from Scholasticism to Personalism.

Heaven

Scholastic philosophers maintained that our ultimate aim is to know being and the theologians therefore conceived heaven in those terms. It consists, they said, in at last knowing being and having one's thirst for knowledge of being completely satisfied. Maritain said that in the beatific vision the soul "enters into the very bliss of God and draws its life from the uncreated God, the divine essence itself, the uncreated comon good of the three Divine Persons".[10] Lonergan said that the beatific vision is knowing *quid sit Deus* or "what God is".[11] Rahner, expressing a criticism, said: "In the famous constitution of Benedict XII on the beatific vision [1336] there is no mention of the Trinity at all. We hear only of the divine essence."[12] This may be a perfect-being theologian's idea of heaven, but it isn't mine.

Personalists believe that we have a desire to know being which will be completely satisfied by contemplation of the divine essence and we also have a higher desire to know persons and to be united with at least some persons in bonds of personal love, by which I mean love for persons as persons and not for persons because of their natures; this

---

[10] Maritain, *The Person and the Common Good*, p. 21.
[11] Lonergan, *Verbum*, p. 203.
[12] Rahner, *The Trinity*, p. 13n. The constitution is in Denziger-Schönmetzer, *Enchiridion*, ## 1000-1001.

love will be satisfied in loving union with the three divine persons, as persons, and this is the highest joy of heaven. Another joy of heaven is union with other human persons or what in our Profession of Faith we call "the communion of saints".

Chapter 14

Sin

The classical problem of evil is: If God is omnipotent and good, how can there be evil in the world? In discussing this we need to distinguish between, on the one hand, troubles that are no one's fault and, on the other hand, moral evil and its physical consequences. This is not exactly the same as the distinction which is often made between physical and moral evil. Only of *moral evil and its physical consequences* should the word "evil" be used, so that if someone is killed in an accident this is unfortunate but not *evil* whereas if a child is sexually molested by a priest, that is evil, not unfortunate, and if someone is murdered his or her physical death is evil. I earlier discussed troubles which are no one's fault and I come now to evil, properly so called.

What sin is

I shall here use "sin" as a theological term. The philosophical term is "moral evil" and "sin" adds something to it. The question is, "What does it add?" Scholastic philosophers maintained that badness is a lack of being[1] and the theologians extended this to sin by saying that the state of sin is the absence of sanctifying grace, an objectively real quality which inheres in the souls of the just. To understand what sin is, however, we need to think about what goes on in the subjectivities of persons who by deliberately and unjustifiably choosing to destroy what they know to be good, and themselves in the process, reject the divine persons and break their relationships with them. It is primarily an I-Thou experience, involving subjects acting as such.

The rejection of a personal relationship can be implicit. If, for instance, a married man has sexual intercourse with a woman whom he meets when he is away from home, he may not expressly intend to be unfaithful to his wife but he is aware of the fact that that is what he is

---

[1] See above, p. 117.

doing. Also, if a woman in a church leaves her handbag on a seat and, while she is going to communion, someone opens the handbag and removes her purse with her money in it, he may not expressly intend to cause her trouble but he surely knows that he is doing precisely that and he implicitly wills it. Similarly, a person may expressly intend to obtain some satisfaction but implicitly know that the action is offensive to the divine persons and that by performing it he or she will break his or her love-relationship with them.

Sin and the Neo-Scholastic ideas of divine control, optimism and foreknowledge

The Scholastic philosophers and theologians maintained that God has complete dominion or control over what happens in the universe.[2] They went on to say that he causes things to happen when he sees that good will come of them. It is difficult to believe this of natural occurences but it is often possible. It may at times be possible to believe it of immoral actions. For instance, if a man looks for a few minutes into a television room in which his teenage children are watching *Othello*, he may later say to them,"What was that terrible thing you were watching last night, in which a big black man strangled a white woman in a nightdress?", and they may reply, "The thing, as you call it, was *Othello*, a great classic, and what you saw was an essential part of it". The thinkers whose view I am presenting said that God is analogous to Shakespeare: he puts into his creation elements which are nasty for him and for us, because they are necessary for it. They said that when God decided to create the universe, from beginning to end, including the Incarnation and Jesus' death, it included Judas, his betrayal of Jesus and his suicide, more or less in the way that if someone decides to stage *Othello* the decision includes Iago's actions and Othello's murder of Desdemona. They say that it is short-sighted to take these elements in isolation and criticise the Creator because of them. Sertillanges said that the more all-embracing our view of reality is, the less evil we see:[3] that is, if we are offended by moral evil in a deep and permanent way we are like the father who saw only the death-scene of *Othello* and because of it condemned the whole play.

[2] See above, p. 155-156.
[3] Sertillanges, *Le problème du mal,* II,50.

Chapter 14: *Sin*

In answer to this it must be said that we might accept the murder of Desdemona in a play but we react quite differently to the real murder of an actual woman. Also, when we consider such things in the past as slavery, the treatment of Australian aboriginals, the Holocaust and the millions of murders in Soviet Russia; and when we consider such recent things as the drug industry, terrorism and crimes of pederasty; it is impossible to believe that they are for the best and that "whatever is, is right".

Scholastics usually shied away from the statement that God *causes* people to sin. They said, instead, that he sometimes *permits* people to sin. For instance, in *Providence* Réginald Garrigou-Lagrange maintained that "everything which comes to pass has been foreseen by God from all eternity, and has been willed *or at least permitted* by him".[4] They went on to say that God permits people to commit sins when he sees that good will come of them, and only then. Charles Journet said: ""If evil was not permitted for the sake of a good, the action by which God permits it ... would be perverse".[5] There are, however, two problems here. First, the word "permit" can be used of a person who sees another being doing something, or about to do something, and refrains from stopping him, her or it; it cannot be used of the person who was the first mover in the operation—for instance, we do not say that Shakespeare *permitted* Iago to deceive Othello, since it was Shakespeare's idea in the first place, and in Scholasticism God is the prime mover and everything is his idea in the first place. Second, the only morally good reason for letting another person do something wrong is that he or she ought not to be interfered with. If, for instance, people see that their unmarried adult daughter is having an affair, they may rightly judge that they ought not to stop her (for instance, by accompanying her everywhere she goes) because as an adult she has a right to her independence; if, however, they judge that she might become pregnant and have a child, and if they regard that prospect with delight, it would be wrong of them *for that reason* to permit the affair to go on, since the end does not justify the means for the interested spectator any more than for the agent. This means that when

---

[4] Garrigou-Lagrange, *Providence*, pp. 216-217.
[5] Journet, *The Meaning of Evil*, pp.103-104.

they said that God permits sins to be committed because of their good consequences the Scholastics attributed immorality to God.

Moreover, if I believe the Scholastic theory and am tempted to sin I can say to myself that if I sin I will know afterwards that what I did was an integral part of creation, which to be as good as it is needed my sin. I will have been like an actor playing Iago in a production of *Othello*, whose contribution, nasty as it is, is essential to the play. Even if God sends me to hell for what I have done, I will be able to say "Thy will be done" to him as I go. I might even, like a certain woman in seventeenth-century France, endow a series of Masses to be said after my death in thanksgiving to God for having decreed my salvation or damnation, as the case might be, for the good of the universe and his own greater glory. Not only that, if someone whom I love is on the way to perdition in this life and the next I can say to myself that whatever happens, and whether he or she is lost or saved, it will be because God decided that it would be for the beauty of creation as a whole. This cannot be right, can it?

Furthermore, consider Jesus' choice of Judas to be one of his apostles. It is said in the gospels that Jesus knew that Judas was going to betray him and the questions arise: Did he know that at the beginning and how certain was his knowledge? According to the Scholastic theory, God in one moment "visualised" the whole story of the universe, from its creation and the fall to our redemption by Christ's death on the cross, and on to what is happening now and what will happen between now and the end of the world; then, like a theatre director deciding to put on *Hamlet*, he made his single decision, as a result of which it all happened, is happening and will happen. Elements in this story were Jesus' choice of Judas, his subsequent betrayal by Judas and Judas's despair and suicide, and because God chose this universe, these things happened. Which means that Jesus chose Judas knowing with certitude that Judas was going to betray him; or it means that the divine persons chose to bring into existence the universe in which that happened. In the alternative theory which I have outlined, Jesus chose Judas not knowing what he was going to do and God the Father did not know that, either; also, what he later saw was that Judas would *probably* betray him. May I say that I regard this as infinitely preferable?

Foreknowledge of immoral acts

The Neo-Scholastic theory of divine foreknowledge was based on the theory of divine control and the idea that one divine decision covers all that happens in the universe and is prior to all happenings. According to this theory, God resembles Shakespeare, who because he wrote *The Tempest* knew before it was produced that Prospero was going to forgive Alonso at the end. God does not need to watch human beings to see what we do, any more than Shakespeare needed to attend a performance of *The Tempest* to see whether or not Prospero would forgive Alonso, but God differs from Shakespeare in this respect: Shakespeare was able to watch performances of his plays, adding observer-knowledge to his author-knowledge, but God cannot watch us and his creator-knowledge is his only knowledge of our actions.

I have rejected the theory of divine control and the belief in foreknowledge that was part of it.[6] I have just offered particular reasons for rejecting its application to sins. The theory which I presented earlier, which is not totally and unrealistically optimistic and according to which there is not one decree in God, there are many, is surely more reasonable.

Impassibility in this context

I outlined above the traditional view that God is impassible and I said that Scholastic theologians gave Aristotelian arguments for it. In this context the question arises: Is God pleased by virtuous acts and hurt by immoral acts?

Thomas said that when God acts mercifully he does not *feel* merciful[7] and Maritain said that we speak metaphorically when we say that creatures please God or give him joy. Preachers and writers of works of spirituality usually assumed that sinners not only choose against their own happiness but offend, which is to say they hurt, God. In the seventeenth century the devotion to the Sacred Heart, in its Paray-le-Monial form, emphasised Jesus' sadness as a result of human neglect and promoted devout prayer before the Blessed Sacrament as a means of consoling him; it also promoted the making of reparation

---

[6] See above, p. 166.

[7] Thomas attributes mercy to God *"secundum effectum, non secundum passionis affectum"* (*Summa Theologica*, 1 21 3 c).

for the hurts that were being inflicted on Jesus.[8] Systematic theologians dismissed as pious metaphor the idea of hurting God. Peter de Rosa was repeating standard teaching when he said in 1968:

> When we sin against God the change and the loss are entirely in us... The loss is all on our side: we suffer the injury and not he. This is what it means to offend or injure God: to be responsible for a situation in which we suffer dreadfully.[9]

In 1986 Richard E. Creel said that his [God's] will is not that we love him; it is that we choose for him or not" so that whichever we choose, "he suffers no frustration of his will".[10] Summing up his position in the last pages of a book, he said that "God has created free creatures that they might choose for or against his kingdom"; if they choose against it, that is in accord with his will and hence "he is not grieved by those who choose against his kingdom".[11] Thus "when we choose for or against God's kingdom, we are choosing for or against our own happiness, not God's".[12] In this matter, perhaps more than in any other, a huge difference existed between what was written in learned books and spoken in lecture halls, and what was written in "spiritual" books and spoken in churches and chapels.

We must, however, distinguish once again between objective reality and subjective experience. That objectively God is pure act and as such impossible to hurt, so that no one can cause God to be less perfect

---

[8] The Society of Jesus committed itself to promoting this devotion and this created a problem for Jesuit theologians, who believed that God cannot suffer and that Jesus in heaven cannot suffer now. Some of them solved this problem by saying that in the Agony in the Garden Jesus foresaw all the sins that were going to be committed and felt hurt by them; he also foresaw the devotion which was going to be shown to him and was consoled by it. This meant that by our devotion now we can cause Jesus to have been consoled on Holy Thursday night. Which was ingenious.

[9] Rosa, *God Our Saviour*, p. 96. If this is true, it must also be true to say: "When we act virtuously the gain is entirely in us.... . The gain is entirely on our side: we benefit and not God. This is what it means to please God: to be responsible for a situation in which we gain enormously."

[10] Creel, *Divine Impassibility*, p 125. On the other hand, Creel says that "free acts cannot be foreknown by God knowing his will or possible worlds" (p. 99), so that he affirms that God observes events.

[11] Ibid., p. 206.

[12] Ibid., p. 145.

Chapter 14: *Sin*

in any way, does not mean that the divine persons are incapable of feeling either joy or sadness.

The stories of two men
I shall now tell two stories, the beginnings of which I shall tell together.

There were two men in Australia, each of whom was intelligent, morally good, married and with a daughter aged seventeen. In each case, an English multi-millionaire, on a visit to Australia, seduced the wife and asked her to fly to England with him, to live with him there, and eventually to marry him. The woman was attracted both by the man and by the prospect of luxury, but she was reluctant to leave her daughter. The rich man said, "She can come with us" and each wife then asked her daughter to go with her and enjoy summers in the South of France, winters in Switzerland, the company of famous people, and unlimited money for anything a young girl might desire. In each case the daughter was thrilled by this prospect and went off with the rich man and her mother. A year passed, during which neither man heard from his daughter. Then both the girls returned to their fathers and said: "It was terribly wrong of Mother to leave you, and it was wrong of me to go with her. At first the high life was so exciting that I managed not to think about you, but before long I could not get you out of my mind and now I have come back, to say I am sorry and to ask you to forgive me." In each case, the father forgave his daughter and she moved back into her old room.

The two fathers were very different and their stories from now on must be told separately.

The first father was an emotionally self-sufficient man who, when his wife and daughter left him, judged intellectually that they had made a bad choice and would suffer for it in the end. He himself, however, experienced no sadness, felt no pain, was not hurt. People who had regular dealings with him in the city saw no difference in him and when someone offered sympathy he said that there was no reason for anyone to feel sympathy for him. When his daughter returned he judged that this was good and took her back into the house. But he *felt* nothing, he did not celebrate, and no one in the city saw any change in him.

The second father was deeply hurt when his wife left him, and hurt in a different, intense way when he learned that his daughter, whom he loved, was going to go with her; and it hurt that he did not hear from his daughter. He was a man of strong character and so did not drink to excess or tell everyone he knew, at length, how badly he had been treated, demanding bucketfuls of sympathy almost every day, and he did his job as well as before; but his friends (who, by the way, were a great help to him) could see that much joy had gone out of his life. When, a year later, his daughter returned, with a flood of emotion he hugged her and told her that he forgave her, completely. Overwhelmed by joy, they both wept. Then they celebrated, laughing uproariously and crying. In the weeks that followed, his friends commented to one another on how joyful he had suddenly become, how often he laughed. He was, they said, more like his own self, though the hurt inflicted by his wife remained.

On metaphysical principles the first man, with his "impassibility", was great whereas the second man was lacking in perfection; but surely the first man was an insensitive monster. It is no wonder that his wife left him, and when his daughter found that he was quite unmoved by her return she probably wondered why she had bothered. The second man was not at all weak or lacking in greatness: in fact, he showed strength in not going to pieces, he showed greatness in generously forgiving his daughter, and in experiencing pain and then joy he showed that he had the great virtue of sensitivity. This shows that the capacity to be hurt by others is not always rooted in limitation of any kind; it also shows that impassivity is an imperfection, whereas sensitivity is a perfection. The highest being is not totally "immanent" or self-centred. To be affected by persons whom one loves is not to gain or lose perfection—it is not to be improved or damaged—and so it is not incompatible with the divine infinity and objective immutability. Let us therefore feel free to say that the divine persons are infinitely sensitive, that they can be moved to joy or sorrow by us when we exercise our free will, and that they are deeply pleased if we love them and hurt if we commit sin.

Conclusion

The denial of divine receptivity is incompatible with the assertion of personal relationships between divine and human persons, which is essential to Christianity. When God is said to be the unmoved first mover, which was Aristotle's idea of the divine being, this sounds impressive until one realises that it implies that when God sees human suffering he is totally unmoved by it and when his love is rejected he is not the least bit upset. This may have been Aristotle's idea but when it is stated now it represents the victory of metaphysics over Christianity.

Chapter 15

Human Beings to Each Other in Scholastic and Personalist Theology

Love of the neighbour

The Scholastic theory

According to Scholastic Philosophy, love is directed towards a being not as a particular individual but as the possessor of a certain nature which two or more beings have in common, and it was said that Christians love one another because they have sanctifying grace in common. It was also said that people love each other not as particular persons but as fellow members of some whole, such as a family, and this was carried over into theology and spirituality, where it was said that a Christian loves other Christians as members of the Church, and other human beings as members of the human family whose Father is God. It was also said that a member of a religious community should not love another member of it in a particular way, but should love all the members of it as his or her fellow religious, and that a parish priest should love all his parishioners only as parishioners.

There is a place for love of others because they are members of a group to which one belongs. For instance, if one becomes a member of a group in a new place, where one is at first a stranger, it is great to find that from the beginning one is accepted, which is to say loved, by the other members. A great merit of this theory is that it affirms the possibility of a universal love, embracing people whom one does not like, people whom one does not know well, and indeed the whole human race.

Another theory

I wish to suggest, as I have done elsewhere, that there are basically two kinds of love.[1] One is the love of persons who, prior to the love, are linked in some objective way. The scholastic theory fits this. The other kind of love is love of persons *as persons,* which is to say as particular individuals, whom one has met. This is found in friendship and in sexual love. Jesus himself manifestly had closer friendships with Peter, James and John than with the other apostles and one may doubt whether this was because of their natural superiority to the others. Also, Christians talk of loving not human beings in general but the neighbour, who by the sound of things is an individual.

That charity is not a separate kind of love

It seems to me that one should not imagine that, for example, a mother should have two distinct loves for her child, a natural mother-love and a supernatural charity, and that a Christian husband and wife should have a natural love for one another and, in addition to that, Christian charity. It seems to me that if people who are Christians have love for other human beings, and if this is integrated into their religious faith, their natural loves of different kinds *are* charity.

The Church

Many Scholastic theologians, who saw value in whole beings, saw the Church as a Big Thing, the locus of supernatural value, standing triumphant, braving storm and earthquake shock, lasting through the ages while its members kept changing. This view tended to be unhistorical because it involved an image of the Church as above history, like a rock that rises out of the sea and stands above its changing currents.

Between World Wars I and II the doctrine of The Mystical Body of Christ became dominant in thought about the Catholic Church. It was particularly popular in Catholic Action movements, since it was taken to imply that clerics and laypeople, whose functions differ in the way that the functions of different parts of the human body differ, are equally members of the Church. In 1943 Pius XII issued

---

[1] See above, p. 126.

an encyclical in which he systematically summed up what had been written about this. In it he said:

> In a natural body the principle so unites the parts that each lacks its own individual subsistence; on the contrary, in the Mystical Body that mutual union, though intrinsic, links the members by a bond which leaves to each intact his own personality. Besides, if we examine the relation existing between the several members and the head, in every physical, living body, all the different members are ultimately destined to the good of the whole alone; while every moral association of men, if we look to its ultimate usefulness, is in the end directed to the advancement of each and every member, for he is a person.[2]

This was Personalist talk. When, twenty years later, the bishops at Vatican II issued a constitution on the Church they began with a chapter on "the people of God", their idea was that the Church at any time is primarily the persons in it. This is a different image from the scholastic one. Avery Dulles says that John Paul II "understands the Church in personalist terms" and in his first encyclical, *Redemptor Hominis* (1979), he said that the Church is "a sign and safeguard of the transcendence of the human person".[3]

In much of the Catholic Church in the first half of the twentieth century, bishops and priests did not commonly use Christian names when talking to one another, many male and female religious had "religious names" which identified them as religious, in some orders of priests a man's friends ceased to address him by his Christian name if he became a superior, and laypeople almost never used Christian names when addressing clerics (among whom I here include brothers and nuns). Now Christian names are far more commonly used than was the case, and what this means is that clerics are seen, first of all, as persons; their roles are secondary.

Also, the Church is not now pictured as a *thing* which is above history but as persons who are in history and Nogar says that "every decree and declaration [of Vatican II] attests to the fact that the Church defines herself and her role in terms of human history".[4] Just as civil government has always been and is now in evolution, so that

---

[2] Pius XII, *Mystici Corporis*. See above, p. 54.
[3] Dulles, *The Splendor of Faith*, p. 189.
[4] Nogar, *The Lord of the Absurd*, p. 93.

no country now has a perfect system which will never change, so the Church's system has evolved and will probably change. To understand it we ought not merely seek to ascertain the timeless truths on which it is based, we ought also to invite historians to tell us the history of the Church as an organisation. Moreover, when a change of some kind is proposed in the Roman Catholic Church a difference often appears between those who oppose it on doctrinal principles and those who argue historically, saying that the present situation is relatively recent and change can at least be discussed. With Personalism there has come a greater historical sense that has changed our thinking about the Church.

Finally, there is now an awareness of the Church as a community of human beings, who experience the sacraments as events in the life of this community. In baptism a person is made a member of the Church, in the sacrament of reconciliation he or she is reconciled with the Church, a marriage is a significant event in the life of the Church, and so on. What forty years ago were called the changes in the liturgy were designed to make people aware of this: for instance, at Mass the people now give one another a sign of peace before receiving communion.

Ecumenism

Finally, a feature of the contemporary Christian scene is ecumenism. It began in the late nineteenth century and led to the Student Christian Movement, the World Council of Churches, and a number of unions of Churches. For many years the Catholic Church kept apart from this but in the nineteen-sixties it joined it and it is surely marvellous. One thing which it involves is a switch in emphasis from "the thing" to the persons in it. When a Catholic cleric met a non-Catholic cleric, he tended to see him as a representative of an organisation which was separate from the Catholic Church as an organisation, and of a community which professed some heretical beliefs. Now he sees the other first of all as a person, who (he supposes) is subjectively sincere. With reference to ecumenism Dulles says: "As a personalist philosopher, John Paul II has over the years had a keen interest in dialogue".[5]

Also, when Catholic theology was thoroughly Thomist, or in any other way Scholastic, it was almost entirely different from non-Catholic theology. In the non-Catholic world there were some protests about the emphasis on *being* in theology. In 1955 Paul Tillich published *Biblical Religion and the Search for Ultimate Reality*, in which he made such a protest and talked about "biblical personalism". He referred to a theology of being which he called ontology and he said:

> The centre of the antiontological bias of biblical religion is its personalism. According to every word of the Bible, God reveals himself as personal. The encounter with him and the concepts describing this encounter are thoroughly personal.[6]

He asked: "Does not ontology request an attitude of depersonalised objectivity, which contradicts biblical personalism in this as in all other respects?"[7] Obviously, fifty years ago he was saying the same kind of thing as I am now saying in this book, and a general remark can be made: Catholic theology is not now as separate from non-Catholic theology as it used to be.

---

[5] Dulles, *The Splendor of Faith*, p. 159.
[6] Tillich, *Biblical Religion and the Search for Ultimate Reality*, p. 22.
[7] Ibid., pp. 54-55.

Chapter 16
Conclusion

Being and person

As I have repeatedly said, Scholastic Philosophy and Theology worked in terms of *being,* producing "perfect-being theology" and defining God as subsistent existence. Also, while Scholastic philosophers and theologians did not deny subjectivity, they regarded such analysis as inferior to the study of objective reality. Personalists, obviously, work in terms of *the person* and their prime concern is subjective experience.

Reduction

Reduction, in the sense in which I am about to use the term, is completely explaining a being of a high kind in terms of a lower kind of being, exclusively. Suppose, for instance, that an amateur theatrical club exists in a country town, run by people who believe in the theatre as an art form. They know that they need to sell enough tickets to cover costs and from time to time they have financial meetings; also, if their designer proposes some elaborate sets and costumes they ask, "Can we afford these?" If, however, a journalist from the local newspaper writes an article about the group and, in the spirit of someone talking about successful films in terms of their grosses, he writes about the group's financial successes and failures, with not a word about its artistic achievements, the members of the group might say: "This article *reduces* an artistic enterprise to a money-making business". Less obviously, if a scientist "explains" morality and religion by saying that they appeared and have survived because they give the beings which have them an evolutionary advantage over beings which lack them, this is *reduction* because it purports completely to explain specifically human phenomena in terms that are appropriate for all animals, including sub-human animals..

It needs to be noted that when a being has several levels within it, the higher level often depends on the lower levels and a complete understanding of it must include an understanding of these lower levels. If, for instance, someone comes to the theatre club above who is thinking of starting a similar club in another town, he or she will almost certainly closely question the club's treasurer and study its balance sheets; and if a book is ever written about the club, while it will be mainly about its artistic achievements it may well have a chapter on the finances, especially if there was a financial crisis at some point. Similarly, completely to understand ourselves we need to study human beings at the animal level and to find out about anatomy, nutrition and genetics. The study of these things is not reductive unless it is supposed that it will lead to a complete understanding of human experience and behaviour.

My contention is that person is higher than being and that to deal with personal activities in terms of being, exclusively, is reduction. Even if being-philosophers say that persons are the highest kind of being, their thought is still reductive, just as if sociobiologists say that human beings are the highest kind of animal and go on to explain them in animal terms, they, too, are guilty of reduction.

In particular, when human interpersonal love is explained in terms of the Scholastic theory of potency and act, which is to say in the terms of a philosophy of being, this is reduction. Also, a classic case of reduction is the Anselmian theory of the second procession in the Trinity: the mutual love of the first two *persons* for each other is excluded and the procession is explained entirely in terms of the self-love of the divine *being*. Another case is the doctrine of impassibility, where the personal involvement of the divine *persons* with men and women is analysed in terms of the perfection of the divine *being*, with shocking results.

Let me emphasise that I do not dismiss the study of men and women as beings, any more than I dismiss the study of human genetics, anatomy and biochemistry. Nor am I opposed to the study of objective reality. I am not ontophobic.

Some statements

Finally, let me repeat some statements which I have made and which are of the essence of what I have been saying:

PERSON IS HIGHER THAN BEING.[1]

SUBJECTIVITY HAS A LIFE OF ITS OWN.[2]

ACCORDING TO SCHOLASTIC PHILOSOPHY OR A PHILOSOPHY OF BEING, ONE IS GOOD, TWO IS BAD AND THREE IS WORSE.
ACCORDING TO PERSONALISM, ONE IS BAD, TWO IS GOOD AND THREE IS BETTER.

---

[1] See above, p. 108.
[2] See above, pp. 108, 126.

Books to Which References Have Been Made

For some books the year of first publication in the original language is given

Allen, E. L. *Existentialism from Within*. London: Routledge & Kegan Paul, 1953.

Beardslee, Claude E. "Personalism and Behaviour". *The Personalist*, 5(1924).
Berdyaev, Nicolas. Dream and Reality: An Essay in Autobiography. London: Bles, 1950.
Bernal, John Desmond. *The World, the Flesh and the Devil*. Originally published in 1929, reprinted Indiana University Press, 1969.
Billot, Louis. *De Verbo Incarnato*. Rome: Gregorian University, 1892. There were many later editions.
Blair, George A. "On Esse and Relatio." *Communio*, vol. 21, Spring 1954, pp. 162-164.
Bonhoeffer, Dietrich. *Ethics*. London: SCM, 1955; Macmillan pb, 1965. This was written in 1940-43.
Bonino, Serge-Thomas. "Théologie Trinitaire." *Revue Thomiste*, July-September, 1992, pp. 756-763.
Bowne, Borden Parker:
———. *Metaphysics*. first edition. New York: Harper, 1882.
———. *Personalism*. Boston: Houghton, Miflin, 1908.
Brasnett, B. R. *The Suffering of the Impassible God*. London: SPCK, 1928.
Briggs, Arthur E. *Walt Whitman Thinker and Artist*. New York: Philosophical Library, 1952.
Brightman, Edgar Sheffield. "Tasks Confronting a Personalist Philosophy." *The Personalist*, 2(1921).
Buber, Martin. *I and Thou*. Tr. Ronald Gregor Smith. Edinburgh: T. & T. Clark, 1937. First published in 1923.

Caraman, Philip. *University of the Nations. The Story of the Gregorian University in Rome from 1551 to Vatican II*. New York: Paulist, 1981.
Clarke, W. Norris. *Explorations in Metaphysics: Being-God-Person*. University of Notre Dame Press, 1994.

Coffey, David. *Deus Trinitas*. New York: Oxford University Press, 1999.
Conti, Charles. *Metaphysical Personalism*. Oxford University Press, 1995.
Copleston, Frederick:
———. *Contemporary Philosophy*. London: Burns & Oates, 1953.
———. *History of Philosophy*, vol. 8. London: Burns & Oates, 1966.
———. *History of Philosophy*, vol. 9. London: Burns & Oates, 1975
———. *Religion and Philosophy*. Dublin: Gill & Macmillan, 1974.
Coreth, Emerich. "Schulrichtungen neuscholastischer Philosophie." In Coreth, *Beiträge zur Christlichen Philosophie*, Innsbruck: Tyrolia, 1999, pp. 385-396. The article was first published in 1988.
Cowburn, John:
———. *Love and the Person*. London: Geoffrey Chapman, 1967.
———. *Love*. Milwaukee: Marquette University Press, 2003.
Creel, Richard E. *Divine Impassibility: An Essay in Philosophical Theology*. Cambridge University Press, 1986.
Cuénot, Claude. *Teilhard de Chardin*. London: London: Burns & Oates, 1965.
Cullberg, John. *Das Du und die Wirklichkeit. Zum ontologischen Hintergrund der Gemeinschaftskategorie*. Uppsala: A.-B. Kundequista Bokhandeln, 1933.

Deats, Paul & Carol Robb, eds. *The Boston Personalist Tradition in Philosophy, Social Ethics and Theology*. Macon, Georgia: Mercer University Press, 1986.
Denziger-Schönmetzer (H. & A.). *Enchiridion Symbolorum*. Freiburg: Herder. 35th edition, 1973.
Domenach, Jean-Louis. "Le personnalisme de Teilhard de Chardin." *Esprit*, March, 1963.
Dulles, Avery. *The Splendor of Faith: The Theological Vision of Pope John Paul II*. New York: Crossroad, 1999.

Ebner, Ferdinand. *Das Wort und die geistigen Realitäten. Pneumatologische Fragmente*. Insbruck: Brenner, 1921.
Existential Personalism. Proceedings of the 1986 meeting of the American Catholic Philosophy Association.

Fairbairn, A. M. *The Place of Christ in Modern Theology*. London: Hodder & Stoughton, 1902.
Fessard, Gaston. *De l'actualité historique*. 2 vols. Bruges: Desclée de Brouwer, 1960.
Fiddes, P. *The Creative Suffering of God*. New York: Oxford University Press, 1988.
Flewelling, Ralph Tyler. "Can Civilisation Become Christian?" *The Personalist*, 1(1920).
Fromm, Erich. *The Art of Loving*. New York: Harper, 1956.

Garrigou-Lagrange, Réginald:
———. *God: His Existence and His Nature.* St Louis: Herder, 1936. Originally published in 1914.
———. *Providence.* St Louis: Herder, 1951.
Geach, Peter. *Providence and Evil.* Cambridge University Press, 1977.
Gillon, L.-B. "A propos de la théorie thomiste de l'amitié." *Angelicum,* 25(1948)3-17.
Gilson, Etienne:
———. *Philosophy of St Bonaventure, The.* London: Sheed & Ward, 1938. First published in French in 1924.
———. *Spirit of Mediaeval Philosophy,* The. Gifford Lectures, 1931-32. London: Sheed & Ward, 1936.
Green, T. H. Prologomena to Ethics. Oxford: Clarendon, 1906. Green died in 1882 and this book, made from his notes, was published in 1883.
Guardini, Romano. *The End of the Modern World.* New York: Sheed & Ward, 1956. This was originally lectures given in Germany in 1948-49.

Hellman, John "John Paul II and the Personalist Movement." *Cross Currents,* Winter 1980-81, 409-419.
Henle, R. J. "Transcendental Thomism, A Critical Assessment." First published in 1981, reprinted in R. J. Henle, *The American Thomistic Revival in the Philosophical Papers of R. J. Henle SJ* (St Louis University Press, 1999).

James, William. *The Principles of Psychology.* London: Macmillan, 1910. First published in 1890-91.
John Paul II: see Wojtyla.
Journet, Charles. *The Meaning of Evil.* London: Geoffrey Chapman, 1963.

Kant, Immanuel:
———. *Foundations of the Metaphysics of Morals,* tr Beck, 2nd edition. New York: Bobbs-Merrill, 1969. This is a translation of *Die Grundlegung zur Metaphysik der Sitten* (1785, of which there are at least four English translations, all with different titles.
———. *Religion Within the Limits of Reason Alone,* tr. with introduction & notes by Theodore M. Greene & Hoyt H. Hudson. La Salle, Ill: Open Court, 1934. New York: Harper Torchbook, 1960.
Keller, Josef M. "De virtute caritatis ut amicitia quadam divina." Xenia Thomistica, vol. 2, pp. 233-276. Rome: Angelicum, 1925.
Kelly, Michael. *Pioneer of the Catholic Revival. The Ideas and Influence of Emmanuel Mounier.* London: Sheed & Ward, 1979.
Kierkegaard, Soeren. *Journals and Papers.* Indiana University Press, 1975.
Knudson, Albert C. *The Philosophy of Personalism. A Study in the Philosophy of Religion.* New York: Abingdon, 1927.

Koblier, John V. "Vatican II as a Program in Applied Philosophy." *The Modern Schoolman,* 75(1997-98)315-327.
Kondoleon, Theodore J. "The Immutability of God: Some Recent Challenges." *The New Scholasticism,* 58(1984)293-315.
Koninck, Charles de. *De la primauté du bien commun contre les personnalistes.* Quebec: Editions de l'Université Laval, 1943.
Lewis, H. D. *The Elusive Mind.* London: Allen & Unwin, 1969.
Ligneul, André. *Teilhard and Personalism.* New York: Deus, 1968.
Lonergan, Bernard:
―――. *Insight. A Study of Human Understanding.* London: Longmans, 1957. Revised students edition, 1958. New York: Harper & Row pb, 1978.
―――. *Method in Theology.* New York: Seabury, 1979.
―――. *Verbum. Word and Idea in Aquinas.* Ed. David B. Burrell CSC. University of Notre Dame Press, 1967. This book was originally a series of articles in *Theological Studies,* 1946-49.

McCool, Gerald:
―――. *From Unity to Pluralism. The Internal Evolution of Thomism.* New York: Fordham, 1989. The sequel to *Nineteenth-Century Scholasticism.*
―――. *Neo-Thomists, The.* Milwaukee: Marquette University Press, 1994.
―――. *Nineteenth-Century Scholasticism. The Search for a Unitary Method.* New York: Fordham, 1989. Originally *Catholic Theology in the Nineteenth Century* (New York: Seabury, 1977).
Mace, C. A., ed. *British Philosophy in the Mid-Century.* London: Allen & Unwin, 1957.
Macmurray, John:
―――. *Persons in Relation.* London: Faber, 1961.
―――. *Self as Agent, The.* London: Faber, 1957.
Marcel, Gabriel. "Remarques sur les notions d'acte et de personne", in *Du refus à l'invocation.* Paris: Gallimard, 1940.
Maréchal, Joseph. *Le point de départ de la métaphysique.* Cahier V. *Le Thomisme devant la Philosophie critique.* 2nd edition, Brussels: Desclée de Brouwer, 1949. First published in 1926.
Maritain, Jacques:
―――. *Degrees of Knowledge, The.* London: Bles, 1959.
―――. *Peasant of the Garonne, The.* New York: Holt, Rinehart & Winston, 1968. First published in 1966.
―――. *Person and the Common Good, The.* University of Notre Dame Press, pb, 1946.
―――. "Quelques réflexions sur le savoir théologique." *Revue Thomiste,* 69(Jan-Mar 1969)5-27.
―――. *Three Reformers: Luther, Descartes, Rousseau.* London: Sheed & Ward, 1944. Originally published in 1925.

———. *True Humanism.* London: Bles, 1938.
Midgley, Mary. *Wisdom, Information and Wonder. What is Knowledge For?* London: Routledge, 1989.
Miller, William D. *A Harsh and Dreadful Love. Dorothy Day and the Catholic Worker Movement.* New York: Liveright, 1973. Reprinted Milwaukee: Marquette University Press, 2005.
Morris, Thomas V. "Perfect Being Theology." *Noûs,* 21(March 1987)19-30.
Mounier, Emmanuel:
———. *Character of Man, The.* London: Rockliff, 1956. Translation of *Traité de caractère,* (1946).
———. *Personalism.* London: Routledge & Kegan Paul, 1952. Translation of *Le personnalisme* (1949).
———. *Personalist Manifesto.* New York: Longmans Green, 1938. Translation of *Manifeste au service du personnalisme* (1936).
———. "Revolution communautaire". *Esprit,* Dec 1934
———. "Revolution personnaliste". *Esprit,* Jan 1935
———. *Révolution personnaliste et communautaire, La* 1935.
———. *Spoil of the Violent, The.* London: Harvill, 1955. Tr. of *L' affrontement chrétien,* 1944.
———. *What is Personalism?* London: Rockliff, 1951. Translation of *Qu'est-ce que le personnalisme?* (1947).
Moltmann, Jürgen. *The Crucified God. The Cross of Christ as the Foundation and Criticism of Christian Theology.* London: SCM, 1974. With new preface, HarperCollins, 1991.
Mouroux, Jean. *I Believe. The Personal Structure of Faith.* London: Geoffrey Chapman, 1959. Translation of *Je crois en toi,* 1949.
Muck, Otto. *The Transcendental Method.* New York: Herder & Herder, 1968. This is a translation of *Die Transzendentale Methode in der Scholastischen Philosophie der Gegenwart* (Innsbruck: Rauch).

Nédoncelle, Maurice:
———. *Vers une philosophie de l'amour.* Paris: Aubier, 1946.
———. *Vers une philosophie de l'amour et de la personne.* Paris: Aubier, 1957. Enlarged version of the above.
Nogar, Raymond. *The Lord of the Absurd.* New York: Herder & Herder, 1998.

O'Collins, Gerald. *The Tripersonal God. Understanding and Interpreting the Trinity.* New York: Paulist, 1999.
O'Malley, John B. *The Fellowship of Being: An Essay on the Concept of Person in the Philosophy of Gabriel Marcel.* The Hague: Nijhoff, 1966.
Ottley, R. L. "Christian Ethics" in Charles Gore, ed., *Lux Mundi. A Series of Studies in the Religion of the Incarnation* (London: John Murray, 1890), pp. 467-520.

Peck, M. Scott. *The Road Less Travelled. A New Psychology of Love, Traditional Values and Spiritual Growth.* New York: Touchstone pb, 1978

Pinkard, Terry. "Analytic, Continentals and Modern Skepticism." *The Monist,* 82(April 1999)189-217.

Quinton, Anthony. *Thoughts and Thinkers.* London: Duckworth, 1982.

Raeymaeker, Louis de. *Metaphysica Generalis.* Louvain: Institut superieur de philosophie, 1931.

Rahner, Karl:
———. *Hearer of the Word.* New York: Crossroad, 1969; translation of first edition.
———. *On the Theology of Death.* London: Burns & Oates, 1961.
———. *Spirit in the World.* London: Sheed & Ward, 1968. Translation of *Geist in Welt,* first published in German in 1939. It is vol. 2 of his collected works in German (1996).

Rand, Ayn. *The Virtue of Selfishness. A New Concept of Egoism.* New York: Signet pb. This has articles written 1961-64.

Regnon, Théodore de. *Etudes de théologie positive sur le mystère de la Trinité.* Paris: Retaux, 1892-98.

Renouvier, Charles. *Le personnalisme suivi d'une étude sur la perception externe et sur la force.* Paris: Alcan, 1903.

Rodriguez, Alphonsus:
The Practice of Perfection and Christian Virtue. Translated from the French. Dublin: Duffy, 1861. First published in 1609.
"Treatise on Conformity to the Will of God", in the above.

Rogers, Carl:
———. *Client-Centered Therapy.* Boston: Houghton Miflin, 1951.
———. *On Becoming a Person. A Therapist's View of Psychotherapy.* Boston: Houghton Miflin, 1961.
———. *Person to Person. The Problem of Being Human.* Walnut Creek, Cal.: Real People Press, 1967.

Rosa, Peter de. *God Our Saviour. A Study of the Atonement.* London: Geoffrey Chapman, 1968.

Rousselot, Pierre:
———. *Intellectualism of St Thomas, The.* London: Sheed & Ward, 1935. First published in 1908. New trans. with Introduction by Andrew Tallon. Milwaukee" Marquette University Press, 1999.
———. *Problem of Love in the Middle Ages, The.* Milwaukee: Marquette University Press, 2001. This is a translation of *Pour l'histoire du problème de l'amour au moyen âge,* first published in 1908, republished Paris: Vrin, 1933, by Alan Vincelette.

Russell, Bertrand:
———. *History of Western Philosophy, A.* London: Allen & Unwin, 1965.
———. *Religion and Science.* Oxford University Press, 1935.

Scheler, Max:
———. *Beiträge zur Feststellung der Beziehungen zwischen den logischen und ethischen Prinzipien.* Jena: Volpelius, 1899. This was Scheler's doctoral dissertation at Jena, 1897, and his first published book.
———. *Formalism in Ethics and Non-Formal Ethics of Values. A New Attempt toward the Foundation of an Ethical Personalism.* Northwestern, 1973. First published in 1916.
———. *Man's Place in Nature.* Boston: Beacon, 1961. First published in 1928, the year in which Scheler died.
———. *Nature of Sympathy, The.* London: Routledge & Kegan Paul, 1954. The book was first called *Zur Phänomenologie der Sympathiegefühle von Liebe und Hass* (1913) and then *Wesen und Formen der Sympathie.*
———. *Ressentiment.* New York: Schocken, 1961. First published in 1912. New edition, with Foreword by Manfred Frings, Milwaukee: Marquette University Press, 1998, 2003 (corrected edition).

Sertillanges, Antonin Gilbert:
———. *Foundations of Thomistic Philosophy.* London: Sands, 1931. First published in 1927.
———. *problème du mal, Le. 1. L'histoire.* Paris: Aubier, 1948

Seth Pringle-Pattison, Andrew:
———. *Hegelianism and Personality.* Edinburgh & London: Blackwood, 1887.
———. *Idea of God the Light of Recent Philosophy, The.* Gifford Lectures 1912-13. 2nd edition revised, Oxford University Press, 1920.

Simonin, H.-D. "Autour de la solution thomiste du problème de l'amour." *Archives d'histoire doctrinale et littéraire du moyen âge,* 6(1931)174-274.

Smith, William B. "John Paul II's Vision of Sexuality and Marriage: The Mystery of 'Fair Love'". In Geoffrey Gneuhs, ed., *The Legacy of John Paul II* (New York: Crossroad, 2000).

Staude, John Raphael. *Max Scheler 1874-1928: An Intellectual Portrait.* New York: Free Press, 1967.

Steenberghen, Fernand Van. *Ontology.* New York: Wagner, 1952.

Stitskin, Leon D.:
———. *Eight Jewish Philosophers in the Tradition of Personalism.* New York: Feldheim, 1979.
———. *Jewish Philosophy: A Study in Personalism.* Yeshiva University Press, 1976.

Tallon, Andrew. *Personal Becoming: Karl Rahner's Christian Anthropology.* Milwaukee: Marquette University Press, 1982.

Teilhard de Chardin, Pierre:
———. *Activation of Energy*. London: Collins, 1970. Essays written 1939-55.
———. *Heart of Matter, The*. London: Collins, 1976. Essays written 1950-55.
———. *Human Energy*. London: Collins, 1969. Essays written 1931-39.
———. *Letters to Léontine Zanta*. London: Collins, 1968. Letters written 1923-39.
———. *Making of a Mind, The*. London: Collins, 1965. Letters written 1914-19.
———. *Man's Place in Nature*. London: Collins, 1964. Book written 1949.
———. *Writings in Time of War*. London: Collins, 1968. Essays written 1916-19.
Thomas Aquinas. *On Kingship*. Toronto: Institute of Medieval Studies, 1949. Thomas wrote *De Regno (On Kingship)* and another author wrote a longer *De Regimine Principum (On the Governance of Rulers)*. These were combined and published as *De Regimine Principum*, which was said to be by Thomas. *On Kingship*, from which I quote, is a translation by Gerald P. Phelan of *De Regno*, which Thomas wrote.
Tillich, Paul. *Biblical Religion and the Search for Ultimate Reality*. London: Nisbet, 1955.
Tonguédec, P. J. de. *Les principes de la Philosophie Thomiste*. Paris: Lethielleux, 1956.
Trueman, Carl R. and R. S. Clark, eds. *Protestant Scholasticism: Essays in Reassessment*. Carlise, UK: Paternoster, 1999.

Varillon, François. *The Humility and Suffering of God*. New York: Alba, 1983. Translation of *L'humilité de Dieu* (Paris: Centurion, 1974) and *La souffrance de Dieu* (same, 1975).

Weigel, George. *Witness to Hope: The Biography of John Paul II*. New York: Cliff Street Books, 1999.
Weinandy, Thomas G. *Does God Suffer?* Edinburgh: T. & T. Clark, 2000.
Whitman, Walt. *Democratic Vistas* in Walt Whitman, *Complete Poetry and Selected Prose (New York: The Library of America, 1982)*. First published in *1871*.
Wilson, A. N. *On Human Nature*. Cambridge, Mass.: Harvard University Press, 1978.
Wojtyla, Karol (John Paul II):
———. *Acting Person, The*. Dodrecht, Holland: Reidel, 1979.
———. *Love and Responsibility*. London: Collins, 1981. Originally a course of lectures given in Lublin in 1958-59; first published in Polish in 1960.
———. *Sign of Contradiction*. Australia: G. Chapman, 1979.

Books Referenced 207

———. *Theology of the Body: Human Love in the Divine Plan.* Pauline Books & Media, 1997.

Wulf, Maurice de. *History of Mediaeval Philosophy.* London: Nelson, 1952. The first edition, in French, was published in 3 volumes from 1900 on. This is a translation of a revised edition which was published in 1924-25.

Index of Persons

Anselm 150-151
Aristotle 22, 24, 34, 161
Augustine 24, 28, 49, 140, 149

Bañez, Domingo 20, 110-112
Beckx 35
Benedict XV 38
Berdyaev, Nicholas 60
Bergson 58
Bernal, J. D. 98
Billot 36, 38, 94, 129
Blackstone 48
Blair, George 159-160
Bonhoeffer, Dietrich 48
Bonino, Serge-Thomas 152
Bowne, Borden Parker 54-55
Brasnett, B. R. 167
Brightman, Edgar 54, 55
Buber, Martin 25, 48, 62, 71, 77-78, 84, 171

Calkins, Mary 54
Cassian 143
Chesterton 39
Clarke, Norris 166
Coffey, David 151
Conti, Charles 69
Copleston 71
Coreth, Emerich 27, 31, 43
Creel, Richard 184

Day, Dorothy 63, 98
Denis (the pseudo) 168
Descartes 25, 141
Dickens 47
Donne, John 96
Dormer, Isaak 167
Dulles, Avery 76, 193

Eucken, Rudolf 58

Fairbairn, A.M. 167
Farrer, Austin 69
Fiddes, P. 167
Flewelling, Ralph 54, 57, 64
Freud 25
Fromm, Erich 125

Garrigou-Lagrange 79, 129, 181
Geach, Peter 160
Gilson 42, 70, 99
Green, T. H. 51, 118
Gurvitch 59

Hegel 50, 51, 56
Henle, R. J., 43
Howison, George 54
Hume 21
Husserl 58

Ignatius Loyola 30, 114
Izard, Georges 62

Jaspers 71
John of St Thomas 29, 31
John of the Cross 143, 171
Journet 181
JP2 19, 45, 69, 73-77, 94, 107, 109, 130, 141, 166, 171
Jung 25

Kant 20, 37, 49, 56
Kant 19
Keller, Joseph 121-122
Kierkegaard 50, 103
Kleutgen, Joseph 34-36, 141
Knudson 53, 56
Koblier 75
Koninck, Charles de 67
Krapiec, Mieczlaw 74

La Mettrie 21
Laberthonnière, Lucien 51
Lacroix, Jean 68
Lactantius 162
Landsberg, Paul 61, 66
Ledochowski 41
Leo X 109
Leo XIII 35, 36, 129
Lewis, H. D. 96
Locke 48
Lonergan, Bernard 43, 83, 89, 115-118
Lotze, Hermann 51
Luther 31, 109

Macmurray, John 72
Marcel, Gabriel 82
Maréchal, Joseph 42
Maritain, Jacques 60, 70, 78-80, 115, 118, 162
Martin 41
Mattiussi 38, 41
Maurin, Peter 63
Maurras 129
Mautner, Thomas 71
Mazella 36
McCool, Gerard 27, 32, 36, 44, 87, 99
McTaggart 52
Mercier 37
Migne 32
Mignot 38
Miller, William 65
Molina 110-112
Moltmann, Jürgen 167
Morris, Thomas 135
Mounier, Emmanuel 61-71, 73, 75, 82, 97, 107, 131
Mouroux, Jean 171
Muck, Otto 43

Nédoncelle, Maurice 124
Newman 34, 35
Nogar, Raymond 44, 99, 191

O'Collins, Gerald 147
O'Malley, John 82
Ottley, R. O. 136

Palmieri 36
Paul VI 76
Péguy 61
Peter the Lombard 29-30
Philo 24, 161
Pius IX 35, 36
Pius XI 76, 129
Pius XII 66, 138, 190
Plato 21, 22, 24, 28, 34
Plotinus 24
Pope, Alexander 159

Quine 20

Raeymaeker, Louis de 94
Rahner, Karl 43, 83-84, 136, 142, 144
Rand, Ayn 21
Rashdall, H. 53
Regnon, Théodore de 151
Reher, Arthur 72
Renouvier, Charles 51
Richard of St Victor 95, 151
Rodriguez 143, 159
Rogers, Carl 72
Rosa, Peter de 184
Rosmini 33, 36
Rosselot 124-125
Rossi, Salvatore 31
Russell 20, 113

Sartre 21, 68, 7
Scheler, Max 57-60, 65, 69, 71, 74, 103, 114, 124
Schleiermacher 49
Scotus 92
Sertillanges, Antonin-Gilbert 156, 164, 180
Seth Pringle-Pattison 136

Index of Persons

Shakespeare 23, 47, 104, 106, 180-183
Sordi 33-34
Stern, William 51
Stitskin, Leon 69
Suarez 29, 31,45,92

Tallon, Andrew 83
Taparelli 34-35
Teilhard de Chardin 80-82
Teresa of Avila 143
Thomas Aquinas 115, 1116, 141, 143, 153, 157, 164, 173, 183
Thomas A Kempis 143
Thomas Aquinas 28, 30, 37, 39, 94, 97
Tillich, Paul 193
Tucker, Abraham 48
Turowicz, Jerzy 65

Vasquez 29

Weinandy, Thomas 161-162
Whitman, Walt 53
William of Ockham 29
Wojtyla see JP2
Wolf 31, 39
Wulf, Maurice de 40

PERIODICALS ETC.
Commonweal 63, 100
Esprit 61, 98, 100
Revue néo-scholastique de philosophie 37
Revue philosophique de Louvain 44
The Catholic Worker 63
The Personalist 54, 69
The Personalist Forum 55, 69

Index of Subjects

Ages of Western culture 22-25
Altruism 57

Being 87

Church 190-192

Ethics 127-132
Existentialism 68, 73, 74, 82, 103

Faith 169-173
Free will 109-112

Grace 175-176

Impassibility 161-162, 183-186
Individualism 57
Indwelling 164
Intellectualism 115-116

Liberal Catholics (19th century) 35
Love 121-126, 189-190

Modernism 37-38, 138

Neo-Platonism 140

Ontologism 32-33
Ownership 128, 13-131

Perfect-being theology 135, 164-168
Persona (the word) 49, 83
Philosophy, notes on 17-26
Protestant scholasticism 31

Reduction 195-196

Scotism 41
Sin 179-187
Slavery 105

Soul 81, 93, 102
Suarezianism 31, 40-42
Subjectivism 65

Takeovers 25
Thomism 45, 78, 89, 144
Traditionalism 32-34
Transcendental Thomism 42-43, 142
Transcendentals (one true good) 119
Transubstantiation 141
Trinity 147-154
Twenty-four Theses 41, 111

Value 113-119